Development of Administration in Assam

With Special Reference to Land Revenue, Justice and Police 1874-1920

M.L. Bose

CONCEPT PUBLISHING COMPANY PVT. LTD.
NEW DELHI-110059

ISBN-10:81-7022-955-3

First Published 1985

Reprinted 2010

Published by

Concept
Since 1974

Concept Publishing Company Pvt. Ltd.
Regd. Office:
A/15-16, Commercial Block, Mohan Garden
New Delhi-110059 (India)
Phones : 25351460, 25351794, *Fax* : 091-11-25357109
Email : publishing@conceptpub.com,
Website: www.conceptpub.com

CONTENTS

LIST OF ABBREVIATIONS

RAA	:	Report on the Administration of the Province of Assam.
RAEBA	:	Report on the Administration of the Province of Eastern Bengal and Assam.
RAR	:	Report on the Administration of Revenue in Assam.
RAREBA	:	Report on the Administration of Revenue in the Province of Eastern Bengal and Assam.
RAJ	:	Report on the Administration of Justice in Assam.
RAJEBA	:	Report on the Administration of Justice in the Province of East Bengal and Assam.
RAP	:	Report on the Administration of Police in Assam.
REJEBA	:	Report on the Administration of Justice in the Province of East Bengal and Assam.
RAPEBA	:	Report on the Administration of Police in the Province of Eastern Bengal and Assam.
ROARA	:	Resolution on the Administration of Revenue in Assam.
ROAPA	:	Resolution on the Administration of Police in Assam.
ROAJA	:	Resolution on the Administration of Justice in Assam.
PGAGD	:	Proceedings of the Government of Assam in General Department.
PGAJD	:	Proceedings of the Government of Assam in Judicial Department.
PGARD	:	Proceedings of the Government of Assam in Revenue Department.

PGFIN	:	Proceedings of the Government of Assam in Finance Department.
PGA	:	Proceedings of the Government of Assam.
PGIHPUB	:	Proceedings of the Government of India in Home Public Department.
PGIHPOL	:	Proceedings of the Government of India in Home Political Department.
PGIHREV	:	Proceedings of the Government of India in Home Revenue Department.
PGIHJUD	:	Proceedings of the Government of India in Home Judicial Department.
PGIFOPOL	:	Proceedings of the Government of India in Foreign Political Department.
PGIHEST	:	Proceedings of the Government of India in Home Establishment Department.
PGIHPD	:	Proceedings of the Government of India in Home Police Department.

GLOSSARY

Bar Barua	:	One of the five higher officers selected from noble families and next in rank to the three great counsellors of the Ahom Kings.
Bar Phukan	:	Ibid.
Bar-Panchayat	:	Higher village Council.
Choudhury	:	Revenue Official. In Lower Assam Revenue Collector was known as Choudhury.
Dulloi	:	Village Headman of Khasi Hills.
Gaobura		Village Elder of the Assam Valley.
Ganak	:	Astrologer.
Got	:	Unit of four Pykes. From the beginning of Ahom rule four Pykes were formed into a Got to serve the State; from the time of Rudra Singha three people formed a Got.
Kakoti	:	Clerks of the Ahom Kings.
Khel	:	A division of people made by the Ahom Kings for specific purposes. Some Khels were vocational. For example, blacksmiths or potters were divided into groups known as Khels and thus there was one Khel for blacksmiths, another for goldsmiths and so on. There were some territorial Khels as well.*
Lal	:	Headman of the village in Mizo Hills.
Lambardar	:	The man responsible for local affairs in Naga village.

*Ibid., p. 26.

Laskar		Village Chief in Garo Hills was called Laskar.
Me	:	Village Council in Mikir Hills.
Mel	:	Council of village Elders or of Royal Officers or Council of the noble of the Ahom community. Usually disputes of local nature were settled by a meeting of village Elders which was known as Mel; the King sometimes consulted important issues in meeting of important officers which was called Mel; and again some relations of Kings had their Councils which also was known as Mel.*
Mouza	:	Revenue Sub-division.
Mouzadar	:	Revenue Collector of a few villages within a Mouza.
Pyaya Sodha Pukhan	:	Officer-in-Charge of Justice. Created during the reign of Rudra Singha, the officer was the sovereign's deputy to hear appeal from Barbarua or Barphukan.
Pyke	:	Subject. Each man subjected to personal service in lieu of tax for enjoying land of the sovereign was called Pyke.
Panchayats	:	Village Council to adjudicate petty disputes of locality.
Rajkhowa	:	Provincial Governor during the Ahom rule was designated Rajkhowa.
Sadiya Khowa Gohain	:	Governor of Sadiya.
Siem	:	Hereditary chiefs of Khasi estate.

*Please see for details—*A Hundred Years of Local Self-Government in Assam*, pp. 23-25.

INTRODUCTION

THE STATE functions through the agency of government. The various departments of the government employ public officials who by law are given the authority of service to the governed and the power to enforce obligations on them. A very considerable portion of the state's wealth is created by the organs of the government and departments are, by their activities, to maintain law and order, increase national wealth and promote national welfare. Administrative history, therefore, is an account of the functions of the various departments of government.

Today, government is no longer confined to police functions. It has a positive part to play in the national life. An elaborate administrative structure has been constructed for this purpose. It defends national existence. It controls the immigration and trade. It attempts to raise the standard of living of all. It assists the poor, the wretched and the sick. It regulates the hours of work. It eliminates dangers and fatigues of labour. It arrests economic depression and mass unemployment. It conserves natural resources. It establishes certain basic standards of morality. It provides amenities and facilities like public administration, art collection, libraries, the encouragement and protection of inventions for the complete development of man. "Government in the twentieth century to a considerable extent expresses the moral sentiment of the community, the responsibility of man to God and the Universe as the Churches did more substantially in the past".[1] Hence the importance of the administration.

A study of administrative history serves a variety of purposes. Administration is a great industry in a sense it spends a vast amount of money and employs millions of persons. Is affects all aspects of the life of man. A second reason is its

1. H. Finer: *Major Governmens of Modern Europe*, p. 6.

value as a form of training in the art of observing and evaluating social facts, weighing arguments and detecting flaws in them, forming intelligent public opinion on public questions and doing various other things which every citizen in democracy is supposed to do. Two and two do not always make four in politics. Sometimes 000 is three in politics. The art of understanding political problems has to be acquired by a study of administrative history and observation of acts of government. Every student of history has noted the regularity with which radicalism and reaction in the government have followed each other throughout the ages. There is a third reason for its study. It is to be found in relation to patriotism. The state demands obedience yet there can be no obedience unless people know what they are to obey. One must learn wherefrom the various institutions and concepts come and one must see what the government is doing at a moment and what course it might take. In part it is a matter of historical fact and partly it is a matter of interpretation. An intelligent being therefore discerns weak spots of the administration.

While approaching the subject we must get rid of the notion that the administration is a simple affair easy to understand without a concentrated effort. It is, in fact, anything but simple. Information that can be had is fragmentary and not often accurate and always tinged with partisanism and more so if the administration is controlled by an alien country. There is a vast body of material in the form of proceedings of the various branches of the government, administration reports, contemporary observations in various works of a secondary nature. It is humanly impossible to go through the details of all these papers. There is only one way by which the study can be made meaningful. It is by glossing over everything that is not relevant and of vital value to the study.

The Development of Administration in Assam 1874-1920 is altogether a new work in the sense that the present work is the first attempt to bring the different aspects of the provincial administration of this province in the campus of a book. So far no scholar has worked onthis subject. But this does not mean that no attempt was made in this direction. The Government of Assam published a pamphlet "An Account of Assam and its Administration" in 1903. But not a single copy is available at present.

The only source of information regarding Assam's administration is the *Imperial Gazetteer* Volume VI, published in 1905. Since then many developments had taken place in Assam. Some specialised works on different aspects of administration or government have come out. An attempt is made to construct a coherent account of these developments up to 1920.

The scheme of the work is as follows. The first chapter gives a history of the province up to the coming of the British in Assam, then how gradually the British formed it into an unit of administration separating it from the Bengal Presidency, the experiment to amalgamate Assam with Eastern Bengal and finally the restoration of the local administration and its ultimate recognition as a province of British India in 1921. The second chapter traces the history of formation of the modern province of Assam that is, administrative divisions and sub-divisions of area. The third chapter deals with the administration of Assam and the Assam Commission. The fourth chapter traces the development of the office of the Chief Commissioner. The fifth deals with revenue administration. The sixth shows the development of the system of judicial procedure, both civil and criminal. The seventh studies the evolution of the administration of police. The last chapter summarises the conclusions arrived at in the previous chapters.

In the preparation of the work a number of obligations were incurred. My first gratitude goes to Dr. N.K. Bose, M.A. D. Phil, Ex-Principal, D.H.S.K. Commerce College, Dibrugarh for encouraging me to do research. Then I express my gratitude to the Ex-Rector Mr. L.P. Dutt, Dibrugarh University, who was generous enough to take me to Gauhati for introducing me to Dr. V. Venkata Rao. I am grateful to Dr. V. Venkata Rao for encouraging me.

I must also acknowledge my debt to Mr. P.C. Sharma, Retired Keeper of Records, Assam Secretariat, Shillong for permitting me to collect materials in his custody. My thanks are also due to Mr. S. Roy, Director of the National Archives and Mr. P.C. Chakravarty, the Librarian of West Bengal Secretariat Library for permitting me to consult relevant papers and books under their custody and Mr. B. Dutta Ray and his magnanimous wife for their generous hospitality during my study in Shillong.

Dibrugarh, the 11 January, 1985 M. L. BOSE

1

HISTORICAL BACKGROUND

THE pre-historic and proto-historic period of Assam is shrouded in mystery and very little is known about it.[1] Mahabharata, Vishnupurana, Kalika Purana and Yoginitantra indicate that in the early period Assam was known as Pragjyotisha and later on as Kamarupa.[2] It was ruled by kings who had the appelation of Danaba-Asura which suggests their non-Aryan origin.[3]

The earliest mention of Assam in historical literature is found in the account given by the Chinese pilgrim Hiuen-Tsang, who visited Kamarupa in A.D.[4] 640. At that time Kamarupa was a strong and prosperous kingdom ruled by a Hindu king Bhaskar Varman. Hiuen-Tsang says that the area of the Kingdom was 10,000 lee from which Winningham infers that it must have included, at that time, the whole of the Brahmaputra valley, Cooch-Behar and Bhutan.[5]

The history of Kamarupa during the period A.D. 640 to 800 is obscure. In A.D. 800 Kamarupa was ruled by Pralambha.[6] The Pralambha dynasty ruled for about 200 years when it gave way to the Palas in A.D. 1000 Ratna Pala was the most noted sovereign of this dynasty. The fall of the Pala power was followed by a period of darkness. After a century and a half, Tingya Deb was replaced by Rama Pala of the Pala dynasty of Bengal.[7]

In the 13th century, a new kingdom known as Kamatapura comprising a small portion of the Kingdom of Kamarupa came into existence. East of the river Manas and west of the river Sankosh there was still a small kingdom called Kamarupa which owed allegience to Kamatapura. East of this Kingdom, the territories were ruled by 12 Bhuyans or Chiefs who had divided among them the valley of Brahmaputra.[8]

The establishment of Muslim power in Bengal affected the course of the history of Assam considerably.[9] There were frequent invasions of Assam by Muslims. The Ahoms made their way into Assam early in the 13th century across the Patkai range. Yet in the early part of the 15th century the Kamata Kingdom under the Khen dynasty was important. The last king of this dynasty Nilambor was overthrown by Sultan Alauddin Hussain Shah of Bengal at the end of the 15th century. But a new dynasty of Koches was established by one Biswa Singh.[10]

The Koches waged a relentless war against the Ahoms for territorial expansion. During the later part of the reign of king Nara-Narayan, the most powerful and glorious king of the dynasty, the kingdom was divided into two with the river Sankosh as the boundary between them. The old dynasty continued to rule with Koch-Behar as its capital but it did not control any territory which now comprises Assam.[11] The new branch of the Koch dynasty with its headquarters at Baruagarh ruled over the kingdom which came to known as Kamarupa. The territory of this kingdom was gradually absorbed by the Ahoms when the last powerful king of the dynasty Parikshit was carried off to Delhi by the Muhammadans.[12]

The invasion of Assam by the Ahoms is a decisive factor in its history. The Ahoms, a Shan tribe wandered into the Brahmaputra valley from Burma about the year A.D. 1226. Once established firmly in the Upper Brahmaputra valley, they followed a policy of expansion and by A.D. 1700 they conquered the territories once included in the kingdom of Kamarupa. About the year A.D. 1655 the reigning Ahom king Chatumla adopted Hindu religion and assumed the name Jaiyadhaja Singh.[13] Towards the end of his reign, the first Muhammadan invasion of Ahom Kingdom took place. Mir Zumla, the Mugal Subedar of Bengal, invaded the Assam Valley in A.D. 1662.[14] The accounts of the struggle that ensued are conflicting but it is certain that shortly afterwards the Muslim army evacuated Assam[15] and Assam did not become a part of the Mugal Empire. In A.D. 1695, Rudra Singh, the greatest of the Ahom kings ascended the throne and he completed the conquest of the whole of Brahmaputra valley. In A.D. 1780, Gourinath succeeded to the throne. During his reign there was the rising of the Moamarias which shook the foundation of the Ahom Kingdom.[16] Gourinath in utter despair appealed to the British for military help. The British had by this time firmly established themselves in Bengal, Bihar and Orissa. Cornawallis sent Captain Welsh with a detachment which succeeded in suppressing the Moamaria rebellion and in defeating Kisen Narayan the king of Old Darrang who had arrogated to himself the sovereignity of the province.[17] In A.D. 1809, Chandra Kanta Singh succeded to the throne. During his reign the Burmese, for the first time, intervened in the internal affairs of the Ahom Kingdom.[18] Chandra Kanta having quarrelled with his minister applied for help to the Burmese. Bura-Gohain after the retirement of the Burmese deposed Chandra Kanta and placed Purandar Singh on the throne.[19] For a third time Chandra Kanta sought the Burmese help but quarrelled with them also. The Burmese expelled him and Chandra Kanta fled to Goalpara to seek British assistance.[20]

Meanwhile, the Anglo-Burmese relation had come to a crisis due to Burmese pretentions over Chittagong, Murshidabad and Burdwan and the English refusing to surrender the fugitives from the Burmese territories. Thereupon the Burmese expelled the British from Sahapuri island, off Chittagong shore, war was declared on them by the Government of Amherst on 5 March, 1824. The Burmese were driven out and the entire valley came under their possession. Meanwhile another British army in Burma advanced upon Prome, the capital of Lower Burma. At Yandabu, General Campbell dictated the terms of a treaty on 24 September, 1825 by which the Burmese inter-alia pledged to abstain from interference of any kind in Assam, Cachar and Jaintia, and recognised Manipur as an independent State.[21] On 22 February, 1826 the British compelled the Burmese to accept the treaty of Yandabu. By this treaty the British acquired the control of the whole of the Brahmaputra valley. It was annexed to Bengal Presidency, gradually, part by part.

Creation of the chief commissionership

For about half a century since the acquisition of Assam by the British it remained a part of Bengal. But it was found that such a diverse country, having peculiar problems of its own and occupying an important strategic position and possessing unexplored potentialities could not be effectively administered as an appanage of Bengal.[22] So, Sir John Lawrence proposed to create a Chief Commissionership for Assam.

Indeed, the administration of Bengal had become unwieldy. All the additions to British territory in Northern India right from the North Western Frontier to the Salwin were practically under its control. Besides, the superintendence of the administration of the Presidencies of Bombay and Madras was also placed under it. Therefore, the Act of 1853 provided for the constitution of Lt. Governorship, and if necessary, a fourth presidency for the better government of these vast territories.[23] A Lt. Governorship was created in Bengal in 1854 to relieve the Governor-General from the burden of the administration of Bengal, so that he could concentrate his attention on all India affairs. But the problem of administering a vast and diverse territory by a Lt. Governor was amply felt. There was no vestige of local-self-government. The administrator had to look after every aspect of human life, besides discharging his general administrative functions. Above all, Government by a single person over a vast territory was not only inexpedient but also dangerous. Therefore, an Act passed by Parliament in 1854 provided for creation, by a proclamation, local administrations, with the prior sanction of the Board of Control and the Court of Directors, in any part of India, to relieve Presidencies.[24] That is, provision was made for the administration of these territories which could not be included in any Presidency or Lt. Governorship. Under this provision Assam was constituted into a Chief Commissioner's province in 1874. On 12 September 1874, the district of Sylhet was separated from Bengal and attached to the Chief Commissionership of Assam.

Eastern Bengal and Assam

Although Assam was separated from Bengal, the territorial jurisdiction of Bengal had grown unweildly with the addition of Bihar, Orissa, Chota Nagpur. And though a Legislative Council was provided, the area was considered by British Administrators too big to be administered by a single person.[25]

They held that the traditional policy of non-intervention was abandoned; reforms which transformed the character of administration were introduced.[26] New Legislation such as the Road Cess Act, 1870, the Census Act, 1872, and new reforms such as the establishment of Statutory Civil Service, the extension of the Sub-Divisional system, the promotion of primary education, the collection of statistics of all kinds, involved a change-over from laissez-faire to a policy of active state intervention for the protection of the less fortunate in the society.[27] The growth of population, the emerging importance of the city of Calcutta, the second city of Empire, the demand for progress in all directions, the important measures of administrative developments which required constant attention, the increasing congestion of business in the Bengal Secretariat, all these made increasing calls upon the time and energy of the Lt. Governor.[28] "It is beyond dispute" observe Lord Curzon in his speech at Dacca on 15 February 1904, "that Bengal must be relieved. No one Government and no administration can possibly devote to nearly 80 millions of people, the personal supervision, care and control which are the objects for which local governments exist. The interest of the people must suffer and they do suffer. . . . No other local government in India administers much more than half the number of the people that there are in Bengal.[29]

Indeed the need for relieving Bengal administration was overdue. As early as 1860 Sir George Campbell suggested that an Executive Council should be created to help the Lt. Governor.[30] The plan was approved by Sir Henry Durand and Sir John Stratchey.[31] But it was rejected on the ground that the officers would not be in a position to dispose of business independently, that there would be waste of time as meetings would be held irregularly and the absence of members would entail unnecessary delay, that there would be lack of continuity and that the project would increase the labour of the Lt. Governor who could otherwise dispose of business at any time.[32] So the burden of administration continued to be heavy. In 1872 Sir George Campbell observed that the two Civil Secretaries who assisted him were more than Secretaries. They were virtually ministers of the Departments[33] committed to their charge. Actually they were so. Four years later, Sir A. Beadon had to appoint a third

Secretary for the administration of finances,[34] and Assam was separated in 1874.

The question of giving relief to Bengal was raised in 1898 in connection with the proposed transfer of the Lushai Hills to Assam and four years later the whole question of territorial redistribution was taken up by the Government of Lord Curzon.[35] The publication of the proposed redistribution raised a storm of opposition. On 18 March, 1904 in a public meeting the suggestion to create an executive council in Bengal and the separation of non-Bengali population from Bengal was requested.[36] It was in fact a revival of the old suggestion of 1867-68 which proposed an executive council for Bengal.

But Lord Curzon in an elaborate explanation emphasised the inexpediency of providing an Executive Council to the Lt. Governor of Bengal.[37] The Executive Council was necessary for guiding the Governors of the Presidencies of Bombay and Madras who came fresh from England without any experience of Indian affairs. But in Bengal it was sure to create dissension among the councillors and that would make the administration stagnant and impotent; the experts would differ in every respect. Further there would be division of authority which would result in weakness and irresponsibility. The Bengal Executive Council might come into conflict with the Council of the Supreme Government.[38] Also the creation of an orderly and efficient government in Bengal would perpetuate the evils from which the administration of Assam suffered and thus retarded the development of that province.

Finally, experience showed that a personal Government and not a highly developed form of Council Government that best suited for India.[39]

It was also suggested by officials and non-officials that Bengal could be relieved by the separation of Hindi speaking tracts and Orissa from Bengal and creating Chief Commissionerships in those territories and Assam could be enlarged if at all by transferring Chittagong division to that province which had been suggested in 1898. Curzon, however, opined that the transfer of Chittagong would take away from Bengal some districts and would thus make Bengal universally unpopular, while the creation of Chief Commissionership of Orissa and

Bihar would make those administrations dependent on neighbouring provinces for the supply of officers. Again, Assam would not be in a position to have a sufficient number of its own officers. The officers on deputation in Assam would leave Assam when they accumulate experience and the new officers coming would find things quite alien. This would stop further development, both territorial and administrative, of Assam.[40] And finally the influence of Calcutta over the people of Bengal would remain as it was and that was an unhealthy system of public organisation which should better have several centres of public opinions.[41]

The Government of India proposed the reconstitution of Bengal. The new province to be called North Eastern Province would consist of a larger part of the Dacca Division, Chittagong division, Cooch-Behar Commissionership, Malda, Rajshahi and Assam, with a population of 31 million. The rest of Bengal would have a population of 54 million. The new province would have a well defined boundary contiguous throughout its length with a well recognised geographical and social distinction. The new province would bring under one administration the typical Muhammadans of Bengal and provide the city of Dacca natural capital for such an aggregation. Moreover, the greater part of lands which produced jute and the whole of tea producing areas with the exception of Darjeeling were included in one province. Finally, the scheme did not involve the breaking up of commissioners' divisions.[42]

The storm of opposition and public discussions were ably met by the Supreme Government. They held that much of the opposition was due to wreckless allegation against tenancy rights and permanent settlement rights.[43] The fear of the loss of national unity of Bengalis was baseless as national unity transcends political boundaries.[44] As for the loss of rights and privileges it was pointed out that the new province would be provided with a Legislative Council and in the place of a Board of Revenue and a Financial Commissioner to implement the proposal of Lord Lawrence.[45] The jurisdiction of the High Court of Calcutta would not be touched till a new High Court was constituted in the new province.[46]

As regards the inclusion of Assam, it was argued that Assam would be benefited by the substitution of Chief

Commissionership by a developed form of administration like the Lt. Governorship. Bengali language would not suffer. In the new province Bengali would occupy a dominating position. Social and educational aspects would not be affected by administrative division. Employment in the new province would be monopolised by the Bengalis. Finally, commerce would not suffer and would find its natural way.[47]

But public criticism raised some financial objections against partition. It was pointed out that the cost of administration would be doubled with the creation of a new province, for 280 more civilians would be required by the new administration. A new Secretariat would be required by the new province. To meet the increased expenditures taxation might have to be increased. The transfer of papers to the new province would create confusions and some might be lost as in 1874, when Assam was created a separate province.[48]

These objections were ably met by the Despatch of the Government of India to the Secretary of the State. The Despatch pointed out that the increased expenditure of Rs. 8.5 lakhs would be met by the revision of Provincial Settlement from the funds of the Government of India, that the amount was worth paying for the inestimable benefit to be derived by the elimination of the evils of congestion in the Bengal Secretariat and the arrested development of the province of Assam.[49]

A close perusal of all relevant documents clearly indicate that the only factors to which the Supreme Government paid attention was administrative convenience and political considerations. The linguistic, cultural, racial, social or ethic consideration of the people involved in the issue were considered as of secondary importance. Particularly the interest of the Assamese and their language were sacrificed on the alter of Administrative necessity. People of Assam of course were divided in their opinion on this question but in general there was unanimity regarding the undesirability of the union of the Bengal district of Dacca, Mymensingh and living with an advanced people like the Bengalis whose impersonal form of administration was not suitable for the Assamese who required the parental care of a personal administration. Even the name of Assam was sacrificed.[50]

The objections of the people of Bengal were refuted by providing the same administration under which they were living but due regard to their linguistic, cultural and social ties with the rest of their folk in Bengal was not given.

On 1 September, 1905, by a proclamation issued by the Government of India, the tracts commonly known as North and East Bengal comprising the districts of Dacca, Chittagong and the Rajshahi Commissionership with the exception of Darjeeling and Malda were separated from Bengal and added to the Chief Commissionership of Assam and thus formed a new Province to be known as Eastern Bengal and Assam. It was placed under a Lt. Governor who was to be aided by a Legislative Council and a Board of Revenue. The jurisdiction of High Court of Calcutta was not affected by the creation of the new province.[51] The Act of 1905 passed left intact the laws which were in force in the areas transferred from Bengal into the new province. The new Province came into existence on 16 September, 1905.[52]

Restoration of the chief commissionership

This was followed by a country-wide agitation. And at last the British Crown declared at the Coronation Durbar held in Delhi in 1911 that the partition would be anulled and Assam would be reconstituted into a Chief Commissionership. Therefore, the Governor General in Council in exercise of the powers conferred by Section 3 of the Government of India Act, 1854 (17 and vict. c. 77) and with the approval of the Secretary of State for India reconstituted the Chief Commissionership of Assam in 1912,[53] consisting of the districts of Kamrup, Darrang, Nowgong, Sibsagar, Lakhimpur, Goalpara, Cachar, Sylhet and the Hill districts.

Indeed before the Durbar took place, the Government of India and the Secretary of State decided the annulment of the partition. The Government of India wrote to the Secretary of State that the creation of the Chief Commissionership would be reversion to the policy of Sir John Lawrence in 1867.[54] He wrote "This part of India is still in a backward condition and more fit for administration by a Chief Commissioner than by a mere highly developed from a government".[55] He further added "anxious as we are to take Bengali feeling into account the partition must be annulled."[56] The Secretary of State agreed to the proposal and communicated his decision to the Government of India that Chief Commissionership of Assam should be revived.[57]

The restoration of the Chief Commissionership in Assam in 1912 clearly demonstrated the fact that Assam had a distinctive role of its own in the Indian Empire. The crude beginning of the province in 1826 as a commissioner's charge had culminated in the establishment of a Chief Commissionership in 1874. The forces let loose by the Chief Commissioner's administration now made it necessary in 1921 to make it a Governor's province. The Montagu-Chemsford Reforms Committee also percieved that developments in Assam had come to such a pass that Assam was to be constituted as a Governor's Province and put on the same footing as other major provinces of India.[58] Following the passage of the Government of India Act, 1919, Assam was constituted into a Governor's Province on 3rd January, 1921.[59]

REFERENCES

1. Gait, E. : *A History of Assam*, p. 1-21.
2. Barua, K.L. : *Early History of Kamarupa*, p. 1.
3. Gait, E. : *A History of Assam*, p. 12.
4. RAA 1905-06, pt II, para 77.
5. Ibid., p. 7.
6. RAA 1905-06, para 78.
7. Gait, E. : *A History of Assam*, p. 35.
8. Ibid., p. 35.
9. Bhattacharya, S.N. : A History of the Mughal North-East Frontier Policy, p. 49.
10. Gait, E. : A History of Assam, p. 44.
11. Ibid., p. 56
12. Ibid., pp. 66-70.
13. RAA, 1874-76, para 107.
14. Sarkar, J.N. : The life of Mir Zumla, p. 232.
15. RAA, 1874-76, pt IIA, para 107.
16. Ibid., para 107.
17. Ibid., para 107.
18. Gait, E. : *A History of Assam*, p. 231.
19. Ibid., p 232.
20. RAA, 1874-76, pt IIA, para 107.
21. RAA, 1874-76, pt IIA, para 107.

22. PGIHPUB No. 517 of October, 1873.
23. Keith, A.B. : *A Constitutional History of India*, p. 137.
24. Ilbert, Courtney : The Government of India, pp. 92-93.
25. PGIHPUB, No. 232 of September, 1874.
26. Ibid., para 115.
27. Ibid., para 115.
28. PGIHPUB No. 166 of February, 1905.
29. RAEBA of 1905-06, para 115.
30. PGIHPUB No. 166 of February, 1905, para 8.
31. Ibid., para 8.
32. Ibid., para 8.
33. Ibid., para 2.
34. Ibid., para 2.
35. RAEBA of 1905, para 115.
36. Ibid., para 115.
37. PGIHPUB No. 166 of February, 1905.
38. Ibid., para 11.
39. Ibid., para 11.
40. Ibid., para 22.
41. Ibid.
42. Ibid., para 32.
43. RAEBA of 1905-06, para 115.
44. PGIHPUB No. 166 of February, 1905, para 27.
45. Ibid., para 27.
46. Ibid., para 28.
47. Ibid.. para 28.
48. Ibid., para 29.
49. Ibid.
50. PGIHPUB No. 157 of February, 1905.
51. RAEBA of 1905-06, para 115.
52. PGIHPUB No. 203 of October, 1905.
53. RAA 1912-13, part II, para 1.
54. Ilbert Courtney : The Government of India, Appendix III, p. 457.
55. Ilbert Courtney : The Government of India, Appendix III, p. 457.
56. Ibid., p. 454.
57. Ibid., p. 465.
58. Report on Indian Constitutional Reforms, p. 128.
59. RAA, 1920-21, part II, para 105.

2

ADMINISTRATIVE AREA

SITUATED between 28.15″ and 24.0″ latitude and 89.46″ and 97.4″ longitude on the North-East borders of Bengal, Assam was the extreme frontier province of British India.[1] Its immediate boundary in 1874 was, on the north Bhutan and the range of hills inhabited by Sub-Himalayan tribes of Akas, Dufflas, Miris, Abors, and Mishmis; on the north-east, the Mishmi hills which swept round the head of the Brahmaputra valley; on the east, the mountain range on the Burmese frontier and the intervening hills inhabited by unsubdued wild tribes, the Patkai range inhabited by Nagas and Manipur; on the south, Hill Tipperah and the Bengal district of Tipperah; and on the west, the districts of Mymensingh, Rangpur of Bengal Presidency and the State of Cooch-Behar.[2]

Formation of modern Assam

The conquest of Assam by the British was an interesting sequel in the history of the Anglo-Burmese war. By article 2 of the Treaty of Yandabu, the king of Burma renounced all claims upon Assam and promised to abstain from all future interference with that country and its "dependencies".[3] The British had declared, when they came to Assam to expel the Burmese, that they would withdraw from the country as soon as peace was restored.[4] But after peace was restored, instead of withdrawing they gradually consolidated their hold over the country. The history of modern Assam, therefore, begins with the British conquest. Its present name also was given to it by its Anglo-Indian administrators.[5]

The consolidation of the British rule in Assam and gradual absorption of its dependencies were sporadic yet continuous. The country was put under Martial Law immediately after occupation and its administration was entrusted to the Officer Commanding. Mr. David Scott, Commissioner of North-East Rangpur, was appointed provisionally, Political Agent and was entrusted with the management of the newly acquired territories and negotiations with the friendly native chiefs.[6]

Mr. Scott had submitted two alternative suggestions, either, the Brahmaputra valley should be restored to an Ahom prince who should pay subsidy to the British or the area as far as Bisvanath should be annexed to Bengal and the upper portion of the province should be restored to an Ahom prince and proper arrangements should be made for the defence of Assam—Burma frontier.[7] But the Supreme Government ordered for the annexation of the entire tract.[8] But Mr. Scott held tenaciously to the idea of restoring an Ahom prince in Upper Assam and as such, evolved a plan of administration the principle of which was to make as little alteration in the existing institutions as possible in Upper Assam while thorough changes were effected in the lower portion.

Mr. David Scott passed away on 20 August, 1831 and was succeeded by Mr. Cracroft to officiate as Commissioner.[10] The Officiating Commissioner discovered the worst possible conditions of maladministration in Lower Assam and suggested the transfer of six parganas of Kamrup to the jurisdiction of the Officer-in-Charge of North-East Rangpur.[11] Mr. Robertson, who succeeded him as permanent Commissioner of Assam proposed the division of Assam territories to the west of the river Dhansiri in five districts, namely (i) North-East Rangpur or Goalpara, (ii) Six parganas comprising of roughly the present subdivision of Barpeta including Nagarberra, (iii) Lower Assam with twenty parganas and nine duars, (iv) Central Assam comprising of Naduar, Charduar, Darrang, Nowgong and Raha and (v) Bisvanath comprising of territories from the river Bharali to Bisvanath including Morang from Kaliabar to Dhansiri.[12] But the separation of six parganas from Kamrup proved inconvenient and were reannexed to Kamrup.[13] Thus terrirtories to Dhansiri from the borders of Bengal were divided ultimately into four districts. Within a few years the districts became popular as Goalpara, Kamrup, Darrang and Nowgong after the names of their respective headquarters.[14]

Meanwhile, the question of rehabilitating an Ahom prince in Upper Assam continued to be discussed. The problem of disparaged conditions of the country ultimately led the conquerors to place Upper Assam under Purandar Singh on 27 June 1833, on condition that he would pay a tribute.[15] But when British authority was consolidated in other parts of the country and people were found satisfied, the bid for resumption of Upper Assam was made. Meanwhile, Purandar Singh had defaulted in payment of his annual tribute and appealed for reduction of the tribute he had agreed to pay.[16] After a tour of the territories, the Commissioner of Assam Mr. Jenkins asked the Supreme Government to sanction the annexation of his territories to British India.[17] The measure was approved by the Vice-President-in-Council. In October, 1938, the territories were formed into two districts of Sibsagar and Lakhimpur and placed under the direct administration of British Officers.[18]

Cachar was originally ruled by an independent native dynasty before the first Anglo-Burmese War. It was invaded by the Burmese, whose assistance was sought by some of the disputants for the throne of Manipur. Govinda Chandra, the Raja of Cachar applied for British help and in 1826, a British force expelled the Burmese from both Cachar and Manipur.[19] On the conclusion of peace in 1826, Cachar was restored to Govinda Chandra who agreed to pay a tribute acknowledging sovereignity of the East India Company.[20] Govinda Chandra, however, failed to subjugate Tularam Senapati who carved out a tract for himself. It was bounded by the Mahur river and the Naga Hills on the south, the Doyang on the west, the Dhansiri on the east and Jamuna and Doyang rivers on the north.[21] In 1830, when Govinda Chandra died without leaving an heir, Tularam laid claim to his territory on an anterior pedigree.[22] But the British formed this tract into a separate district and placed it under a Superintendent in August, 1832.[23] Tularam, however, was given a pension of Rs. 50 per month. He was deprived of the title of Raja and the right to administer justice except tribal cases.[24] In 1833, the rest of Cachar was added to the British territory.[25]

Matak, the tract south of Sadiya, was given to a Chief called Bar-Senapati, who had protected its people from Burmese atrocities, on condition of supplying paiks which was later converted into a monetary payment.[26] The Bar-Senapati died in 1839, nominating his son Maju Gohain as his successor. But the latter refused the new terms offered to him whereupon the tract was annexed to the British territory.[27] In 1842, by a formal proclamation, Matak and Sadiya were incorporated into the British territory and were subsequently added to the Lakhimpur district, the headquarters of which was transferred to Dibrugarh in the Matak country.[28]

Sadiya was placed under a Khamti Chief who swore fealty to the English.[29] But in 1835, a dispute arose between the Sadiya Khowa Gohain and Bar-Senapati regarding a tract of land.[30] The Political Agent at Sadiya attached the land in question called the disputants to appear before him to prove their claims.[31] The new Sadiya Khowa Gohain forcibly occupied the land without appearing before the Political Agent.[32] The British abolished the post of Sadiya Khowa Gohain and placed Sadiya under their control in Lakhimpur district.

While these developments were taking place, the local officers of the semi-independent tribal tracts of Khasi Jaintia Hills found it necessary to bring these tracts under the immediate control of the British. Nunklow, in the Khasi Hills, was acquired by the British for the residence of some British subjects in 1826 under treaty with the Raja.[34] The Raja had agreed to allow a road to be constructed across the Hills to connect Cachar and Sylhet with the Assam Valley.[35] A misunderstanding arose between the officers engaged in the construction of the road and the local people in 1829. Some of the officers were massacred. Troops were despatched in January, 1833 to punish the culprits.[36] The Khasi Chief Tirat Singh surrendered himself to the Company. A Political Agent was appointed for general superintendence over Khasi and Jaintia Hills.[37] Again in 1832, four British subjects were seized by the Raja of Gobha, a vassal of Jaintia King, and offered them as a sacrificeat the shrine of Goddess Kali.[38] One of them escaped to tell the tragedy of his fellow companions. At this juncture, Ram Singh, the Jaintia Raja died and his successor, Rajendra Singh, declined to hand over the culprits to the British.[39] Thereupon, the Political Agent, by a proclamation, annexed the Jaintia parganas to the British territories and incorporated them into the district of Sylhet.[40] A few weeks later Gobha was similarly annexed to Nowgong.[41] But the Hills remained under the Political Agent at Jowai and the Raja was pensioned off.[42]

Three thanas of Goalpara, Dhubri and Karaibari, originally formed part of the district of Rangpur of the province of Bengal.[43] By regulation X of 1822, they were separated from the Rangpur district, and were freed from the operation of General Regulations.[44] They were placed under a special system of Governmet like that of the Garo Hills.[45] The new tract was called North-East Rangpur. Mr. David Scott was appointed as its first Civil Commissioner. When Assam was constituted into a Commissioner's circuit in 1826, this trace was included in it.[56] It continued to be a part of Assam till 1867. In 1867, when the Cooch-Behar Commissionership was formed, the North-East Rangpur along with Eastern Duars which were obtained from the Bhutias in 1866 were made parts of it.[47] In 1848, judicial administration of the Garo Hills and Goalpara were transferred to the Judicial Commissioner of Assam, though their administration remained in the hands of the Commissioner of Cooch-Behar. In 1874, when Assam was constituted into a Chief Commissionership, Goalpara and Eastern Duars were transferred to it.[49]

The Garo Hills were a part of the Goalpara district till 1866.[50] In that year a special Civil Commissioner was appointed to look after its administration. This did not improve matters.[51] So, an officer was stationed at Tura, instead of at Goalpara. The system of administration devised by him was satisfactory. In 1869, it was separated from Goalpara and constituted into a separate administrative district.[52]

The tribes inhabiting the Naga Hills were commonly known as Nagas. But they spoke different dialects and each had a distinctive name of its own. The British Government did not wish to bring the Naga Hill areas under their direct administration.[53] The Policy of the Government was to contain these tribes within their areas, non interference in their internal affairs and close the markets in the neighbouring areas in case they misbehaved.[54] But the chronic atrocities perpetrated by the Angamis compelled the British to station an officer at Asalu in 1854 and establish a line of frontier posts.[55] Subsequently, the Angami tract was formed into a district with headquarters at Samaguting which was later shifted to Kohima in 1878.[56] Since then the policy followed by the British was penetration and incorporation of tribal areas into the British territory, in 1875, the Lotha Naga territory, in 1889, the Ao Naga territory and in 1917 the Kuki Naga tracts were added to the district.[57]

Lushai Hills stretched from south-east of Assam to Chittagong. The southern tracts were inhabited by the Kukis. Later on the Lushais became masters of the hills and the Kukis were driven to the northern fringes.[58] In 1860, the Bengal Government passed Act XXII for the administration of the Bengal portion of the Kuki Hills and the results were satisfactory.[59] The North Lushai Hills in Assam were a constant source of trouble. So Political Officers were posted at Aijal and Lungleh in the nineties. In 1893, the Government of India proposed the amalgamation of the two portions of the Kuki tracts of the Bengal Government and Assam.[60] In 1898, these were combined and placed in charge of a Superintendent and transferred to the control of the Chief Commissioner of Assam.[61]

Besides these districts, Assam Administration had the charge of twenty-five major hill tribes inhabiting over 33,000 square miles of territory along the southern slopes of Himalaya.[62] The Bengal Frontiers Tract Regulation V of 1873 was provided for the drawing of an Inner Line, travel beyond which was restricted.[63] In 1880, Assam Frontier Tract Regulation was issued "to provide for the removal of certain enactments from the Frontier Tracts inhabited by the barbarous tribes.[64] This was supplemented by another in 1884.[65]

These wide tracts of territory were divided by a Government of India Notification into three administrative units in 1914. These were : (i) The Central and Eastern Section, (ii) Lakhimpur Frontier Tract, and (iii) Western Section.[66] The first and third were placed under the charge of a Political Officer in 1914, while the second unit was placed under the Deputy Commissioner of Lakhimpur district. The Headquarters of the Central and Eastern Sections was located at Sadiya and those of the Western at Charduar.[67] In 1919, the Central and

Eastern Sections were renamed as Sadiya Frontier Tract and Balipara Frontier Tract.[68] The administrative control of these areas was vested in the Administration of Assam.[69]

The territories of Assam Commission thus consisted of six districts of the Brahmaputra Valley, namely, Goalpara, Kamrup, Nowgong, Darrang, Sibsagar, and Lakhimpur and Lushai tracts, Naga Hills, Jaintia and Khasi Hills and Garo Hills besides the Frontier tracts of North-East Frontier.

The inconvenience of administering such a diverse territory as an appanage of Bengal was keenly felt in the sixties of the nineteenth century.[70] In 1874, it was separated from Bengal when Sylhet was transferred to Assam Commission from Dacca Division of Bengal Government.[71] When the Government of India Act 1919 was promulgated in 1921, the same territories constituted the Governor's province of Assam.

Physical features

The valley of Brahmaputra was a long alluvial plain, about 450 miles long, and of an average width of 50 miles.[72] It was shut in by mountains on the north, east and south, with the Brahmaputra flowing through its entire length from east to west. Countless tributary streams of every magnitude, fell into the Brahmaputra from the bordering mountains on either side. The uniform level of the valley was intercepted by a few low conical hills, projecting like spurs. The converging hills at Goalpara appeared almost to shut in the Assam Valley and for this the place was known as the Gate of Assam.[73]

One of the principal characteristics of the Brahmaputra, attributable perhaps to the large amount of silt brought down by it, was its tendency to change its course.[74] In the Assam Valley its encroachments though at times was considerable were limited by the hills, but the deviations of its lower course had been most remarkable.[75]

The valley of Surma comprised of the two districts of Sylhet and Cachar. It was a flat alluvial plain of 125 miles long and 60 miles wide.[76] On the north the valley was shut in by the Khasi and Jaintia Hills and the Naga Hills, on the east by the Manipur Hills which form the watershed dividing the water systems of eastern Bengal from that of Irrawaddy and on the south lay the

Lushai and Tipperah Hills and their offshoots westward from the same range.[77]

The western and eastern portions of the Surma Valley differed considerably in their physical features. The western portion, comprising of the district of Sylhet, for the most part was a large alluvial plain, averaging some 70 miles in width, with clusters of low sand, hillock, locally termed, 'Tilas' scattered here and there. It was traversed by numerous streams and watercourses, running principally from west to east, whose margins in many cases were somewhat more elevated than the surrounding country.[79] Consequently during the rainy months of the year, from about June to October, the whole of the district with the exception of the hillocks and the villages built on the elevated banks of the rivers, or artificially raised places, remained under water. In the south, however, the country became somewhat hilly, being penetrated by several spurs running out from the higher ranges in Hill Tipperah. In the centre of the district a detached range of hills cropped up, called the "Ita Hills". All these hills were covered with dense jungle.[80]

In its eastern portion consisting of the district of Cachar, the valley narrowed, and presented very diversified features. Low detached spurs and offshoots from the main hilly tracts which bend the valley on both north and south covered mostly more or less with dense jungle, extended almost to the river's edge on either side, with rich alluvial valleys between them.[81] Most of the low lands in these villages remained under water during the rains.[82]

The Surma or Barak River, came down from the chain of mountains to the north of Manipur.[83] After flowing for about 180 miles through a mountainous country, it became navigable for boats of burden about 20 miles above Banskandi, a village in Cachar, and passing across that district, divided into two branches at Bariga, the eastern limit of Sylhet district.[84] One branch flowed nearly due west, by the town of Sylhet and Chhatok, and fell ultimately into the Megna.[85] The second branch called Kasiara, flowed diagonally across the Sylhet district in a south westernly direction, and reunited with the northern branch near Lakki, about 26 miles above its junction with the Megna.[86]

The Naga Hills, Khasi and Jaintia Hills, and Garo Hills, were a continuation of the mountainous chain which swept on the northern side, with a more gradual slope on the south.[87] The intervening valley was very narrow. The major portion of the whole tract was uncultivated, and was covered with dense jungle under growth. In the higher hills there was cultivation on the southern faces. Further west wards, the hills were more rugged and abrupt.[88] The main ridge, named the Barrail, in the neighbourhood of Samagutting was remarkably precipitious in character, and toward to the height of 10,000 feet. On the western slope of this ridge a good deal of terraced rice cultivation was carried on by the Nagas. In other parts the cultivation was exceedingly spares.[89]

The peculiar feature of the Khasi and Jaintia range of hills was the abruptness with which they rose almost perpendicularly from the Surma Valley on their southern face, attaining rapidly an altitude of over 4,000 feet, while on the north side the ascent from the Assam Valley was by a succession of gradual spurs and detached ridges.[90] The lower portions of the hills on both sides were clothed in dense forest and jungle. The upper plateau and main central tracts consisted of a succession undulating downs, broken here and there by the deep valleys of the large hill streams, and covered of forest by the migratory cultivation of the inhabitants, except where a few sacred groves escaped the general devastation.[91] Shillong, which was situated about the centre of this tract, stood at an elevation of 4,900 feet, while the ridge overlooking it, was 6,449 feet above the sea and was the highest of any part of the range.[92]

The Garo Hills was the termination of this chain of hills and presented very similar characteristics.[93] They were set up and precipitious on the southern face, sloping in gradual ridge to the plains on the northern and western sides. They were of rather lower general elevation, the highest peak of the range, below which Tura, the Headquarters of the district was situated, being not more than 4,700 feet above sea level.[94] Tura itself had an elevation of only 1,300 feet.[95]

The lands in Assam could be divided into three general classes.[96] The first division consisted of the mountains and hill ranges which again could be subdivided into three sections.

First, the great mountain chains, independent group of hills, and lastly, isolated hills and hillocks. The second class consisted of hills lying in groups, large and small, on the plains of the Brahmaputra Valley, and forming either independent units by themselves or continuations of the northern or southern ranges The largest group was that of the Mikir Hills. The third division of the land was what might be called "the diluvial plain of the valley, its level being generally above the ordinary innundation of the Brahmaputra and of its tributaries".[97]

The soil of Assam greatly varied in character.[98] The greater part of the territory west of the Sankosh river consisted of a mixed free soil, which was ash colour and singularly uniform in character, and consisted of light friable loam, superimposed on a deep bed of pure sand. The soil on the Brahmaputra Valley, though varied at places, was on the whole exceedingly fertile, and well adopted to all kinds of agricultural purposes. For the most part it was composed of a rich black loam, reposing on a gray sandy, clay, though occasionally consisting of a light yellow clayish texture.[99]

In Sylhet, the soil was for the most part, blue clay, which was black on the borders of the bills or hoars.[100] The low isolated hillocks, or tilas were composed of soft sandstone. In Cachar Plains the soil was an alluvial deposit of sandy soil.[101] The several groups of hills situated in the valley were of granite formation, the granite containing frequently veins of quartz, in conjunction with metamorphosed. The surface soil of these hills were a rich sandy loam, while the surface soil of the hillocks and moulds of the districts of Sylhet and Cachar was of a rich vegetable mould.[102]

The climate of the province of Assam, both in the Brahmaputra and Surma Valley was noted for its extreme humidity.[103] Besides continuous rain in season which commenced in March and ended in October, occasional showers occurred althrough the year. At Cherrapoonjee, which was situated at the south edge of the Khasi Hills, immediately over looking the plains of Sylhet, the rainfall was notorious for its excessive amount (500" per annum).[104] Yet the Brahmaputra Valley enjoyed a far more equitable temperature than was generally through out India, the warm weather there being very moderate and nights throughout the year cool and refreshing. Nevertheless, its climate had always been far from salubrious.[105]

The territories thus brought under the province of Assam in 1874 covered an area of 41,798 square miles of directly administered territories.[106] The population was estimated to be 14,150,000 souls and revenue to be Rs. 52,50,000.[107] The total area in 1920 increased to 77,500 square miles and population rose to 7,990,246 persons.[108] The revenue of Assam amounted to Rs. 2,28,04,949, but the expenditure of the Local Administration had also mounted to Rs. 2,06,89,377.[109] Thus the territory of the province as well as the population were inadequate to make a case for separate province for Assam. Smallest of the Indian provinces, it justified its separate Local Administration for its peculiar necessities, strategic location and undeveloped potentialities though neither administrative area nor population nor revenue of the province warranted it in 1874.[109]

REFERENCES

1. RAA 1874-76, part I, para 1.
2. Ibid.
3. Aitchinson, C.U. : Treaties, etc. Vol. II, p. 230.
4. Barpuzari, H.K. : *Assam in the Days of the Company*, p. 13.
5. Bamah B. and Deo shai Pharku NN edited, Ahom Lexior. p. 197-98.
6. Bhuyan, S.K. : *Anglo-Assamese relations*, p. 528.
7. Lahiri, R.M. : *The Annexation of Assam*, p. 29
8. Ibid., p. 32.
9. Ibid., p. 56.
10. Barpuzari, H. K. : *Assam in the Days of the Company*, p. 61.
11. Ibid.
12. Ibid., p. 66.
13. Ibid., p. 67.
14. Ibid., p. 67.
15. Lahiri, R.M. : *The Annexation of Assam*, p. 117.
16. Ibid., p. 175.
17. Ibid., p. 179.
18. Gait, E. : *A History of Assam*, p. 360.
19. RAA 1874-76, part II, p. 115.
20. Gait, E. : *A History of Assam*, p. 341-42.
21. Ibid., p. 342.
22. Barpuzari, H.K. : *Assam in the Days of the Company*.

23. RAA, 1874-76, part II, para 115.
24. Lahiri, R.M. : *The Annexation of Assam* p. 198.
25. RAA, 1874-76, part II, para 115.
26. Gait, E. : *A History of Assam*, p. 341.
27. Lahiri, R.M. : *The Annexation of Assam*, p. 205.
28. Gait, E. : *A History of Assam*, p. 362.
29. Lahiri, R.M. : *The Annexation of Assam*, p. 208.
30. Ibid.
31. Gait, E. : *A History of Assam*, p 344.
32. Lahiri, R.M. : *The Annexation of Assam*, p. 208.
33. Ibid.
34. RAA 1874-76, part II, para 118.
35. Ibid.
36. RAA 1874-76 part II, para 17.
37. Ibid., para 118.
38. Ibid., para 117.
39. Gait, E. : *A History of Assam*, p. 358.
40. Ibid., p. 358.
41. RAA 1874-76, part II, para.
42. Gait, E. : *A History of Assam*, p. 358.
43. Ward. : The Assam Land Revenue Manual, p. XLI.
44. RAA 1920-21, part II, para 99.
45. Ibid.
46. Ibid., para 80.
47. Ibid.
48. Wa-d : The Assam Land Revenue Manual, p. XLI.
49. Ibid.
50. RAA 1874-76, part II, para 122.
51. Ibid., para 120.
52. RAA 1874-76, part II, para 120.
53. Chakraborty, B.C. : *British Relation with Hill Tribes*, p. 38.
54. Ibid
55. RAA 1874-76, part II, para 122.
56. Ibid.
57. Chakraborty, B.C. : *British Relation with Hill Tribes*, p. 83.
58. RAA 1874-76, part, II, para 122.
59. Ibid.
60. RAA 1920-21, part II para 103.
61. Ibid.
62. Assam Sahitya Sabha : The Outlook on NEFA, p. 1.
63. Choube, S.K. : *Origin and Development of the Administration of NEFA*.
64. Chakraborty, B.C. : *British Relation with the Hill Tribes of Assam*, p. 194.
65. Choube, S.K. : *Origin and Development of the Administration of NEFA*.

66. Col. Luthra, P.N. *Constitutional and Administrative Growth* of *NEFA*.
67. Ibid.
68. Choube, S.K. : *Origin and Development of the Administration* of *NEFA*.
69. Ibid.

    N.B. : Both Dr. S.K. Choube, Lecturer, Saint Edmund's College, Shillong and Col. P.N. Luthra, Advisor to the Governor of Assam for NEFA presented the papers quoted above at a Seminar held in Shillong in November, 1969.
70. Supra, pp. 5-6.
71. Ibid.
72. RAA 1874-76, part I, para 2.
73. RAA 1874-76, part I, para 3.
74. Ibid., para 6.
75. Ibid., para 6.
76. Ibid., para 7.
77. Ibid., para 7.
78. RAA 1874-76, para 8.
79. Ibid.
80. Ibid.
81. Ibid., para 9.
82. Ibid.
83. RAA 1874-76, para 10.
84. Ibid.
85. Ibid.
86. Ibid.
87. Ibid., para 11.
88. Ibid., para 12.
89. RAA 1874-76, part I. para 12.
90. Ibid., para 13.
91. Ibid., para 12.
92. Ibid.
93. RAA 1874-76, part I, para 13.
94. Ibid.
95. Ibid.
96. Ibid., para 14.
97. Ibid., para 15.
98. RAA 1874-76, part I, para 16.
99. Ibid.
100. Ibid., para 17.
101. Ibid.
102. Ibid.
103. RAA 1874-76, part I, para 22.
104. Ibid., para 33.
105. Ibid., para 22.

106. Ibid., para 1.
107. PGIHPUB No. 533 of October, 1873.
108. Census of India Report Vol. III, part I, para 4.
109. RAA 1920-21, part II, para 172.

3

ASSAM ADMINISTRATION AND COMMISSION

CENTRALISATION of Administration of Indian territories of the East India Company began in 1773 when the Regulating Act was passed by the British Parliament.[1] The Charter Act of 1833 carried the process of centralisation one step further.[2] By Section 39 of the Act the superintendence, direction and control of the whole civil and military Government of all the territories and revenues of India were vested in the Governor-General of India in Council. It was also given all the powers of Government over all parts of India and held responsible for good Government in them all.[3]

But with the expansion of the empire, the Government of Fort—William was over burdened and provisions for providing Local Administrations were mooted. The Government of India Act 1854 empowered the Governor-General of India in Council to create Local Administration for any territory.[4] In the eye of law Governor-General was the Local Government for those areas as long as he did not delegate his powers.[5] Under this Act, Assam was made a Chief Commissioner's province.

The Local Administrations had no legal powers, but merely exercised the authority delegated to it by the Supreme Government. It could not create any new office and impose any new tax without the approval of the Supreme Government.[6] Its main concern was to maintain law and order, collect the taxes and dispense justice.

Scheme of the chief commissioner's administration

As regards the scheme of administration for Assam, the Secretary of State wrote to the Governor-General: "I am of opinion, however, that the system of administration ought at first to be as simple and inexpensive as possible. I doubt whether all the usual staff of secretaries and departments usually attached to a Chief Commissioner in more advanced province need to be established in connection with office in Assam".[7]

The Government of Bengal also gave a sketch of the new administration to be provided for Assam. They suggested that between the Chief Commissioner and the Deputy Commissioners in charge of the districts there should not be a Divisional Commissioner.[8] The small districts might be converted into subdivisions but if Divisional Commissioners were appointed, the Sub-Divisions might be converted into districts. They also suggested to retain the jurisdiction of the High Court of Calcutta over Assam. The Judicial Commissioner of Assam and the Judge of Sylhet were to continue as Civil and Sessions Judges of Assam Valley and Sylhet and Cachar respectively. The Judges were to be under the High Court of Calcutta for judicial purposes but subordinate courts were to be placed under the Chief Commissioner of Assam.[9]

The Government of India was influenced by the suggestions made by the Secretary of State and the Lt. Governor of Bengal in the formulation of the administrative set-up for the province. They proposed to the Secretary of State in Council that Chief Commissioner would be placed at the helm of affairs with full powers of office.[10] There should be no full Secretariat establishment but a Secretary only would be placed at the top of the existing Commissioner's establishment. A Judicial Commissioner to supervise the works of the Lower Courts might be appointed. He might be provided with an Inspector General of Police and Jails. If no Judicial Commissioner was appointed his salary would be paid to inspecting officers. But Government by departments would be avoided as far as possible and all administrative authority would be vested in the Chief Commissioner. They suggested to take over, the officers, their names, and their functions from Regulation to Non-Regulation pattern.[11]

Accordingly, the executive authority of the Local Administration of Assam was vested in the Chief Commissioner himself.[12] At first he was provided with the assistance of a Secretary. But no departmental officer was provided to take care of, and advise the Chief Commissioner on different aspects of the administration.[13] The Chief Commissioner was to undertake the inspection of the different branches of administration and attended to all the enquiries and references of his subordinates. Only the Public Works Department was under the charge of a Chief Engineer and Forest and Medical Departments continued to be administered by the Bengal Government.[14]

The Headquarters of Local Administration was located at Shillong.[15] The Headquarters of the Commissioner of Assam was at Gauhati. But the Chief Commissioner of Assam argued that the addition of the Surma Valley had rendered Gauhati a far off place. Habitable land around was not enough to accommodate the expanding establishment of the provincial administration. Moreover, the climate of Gauhati was most unsuitable for the European Officers.[16] Shillong, on the hills, at an altitude of 5,000 feet above the sea leve! was cool throughout the year. In winter, the cold was not too severe. Moreover, during winter the Chief Commissioner went on tour. So the administrative affairs were not neglected. As a matter of fact, throughout the year, the administration was looked after. Shillong as Headquarters above all enabled the Chief Commissioner to keep a watchful eye on both the valleys.[17]

The location of the capital, however, was considered on administrative grounds particularly with a view to suppress quickly possible outbreak or rebellion. The convenience of the people were not taken into consideration. Shillong was situated at a distance of 350 miles from north-east corner of the Lakhimpur district and not less than 200 miles to the south from boarder of Bengal. In those days of undeveloped transport facilities, when people had to depend on mainly slow moving steam ships, they could hardly come to the centre of administration in case of necessity. Moreover, in rainy season when the Head Assistants were responsible for the completeness and accuracy of their subordinates.[18] The Secretary allocated worked to appropriate branches. Confidential papers were, however, dealt with by the Superintendent or the Head Assistants.[19]

The Commissioner of Assam had four departments, e.g. Judicial, Revenue, Police and Native. In the Judicial department there were one Head clerk and four other assistants; in Revenue department there were one Head clerk and four assistants; in Police department there were a Head clerk and a Second clerk but there were three Duftries; and in the Native department there were one Sherestadar and four Muharrirs in addition to two additional clerks. Besides, there were one Sweeper and one Bhistee.[20] The Chief Commissioner was provided with nine more clerks besides some menials as desired. Thus the Secretariat of the Province in 1874 consisted of a Secretary and an Assistant Secretary, three Head Assistants one each for General, Judicial and Revenue departments, one Record Keeper, eleven clerks, one Registrar, one Recorder, one Despatcher, eight copyists, and one Draughtsman. For the Native department which dealt with the settlement works there was a Sherestadar, one Muharrir, one book Binder, two Duftries, and six Chaprasis. Besides, there were one Sweeper and one Classie. The Secretary was provided with one Jamadar and three Chaprassis and the Assistant Secretary was provided with three Chaprassis. Thus the Assam Commissioner's establishment was converted into a Secretariat without much change.[21] Expenditure did not increase materially. In 1873 the Commissioner's establishment increased considerably and expenditure amounted to Rs. 2,133. When converted to Chief Commissioner's Secretariat in 1874, the expenditure rose to Rs. 4,540 only.[22]

By May, 1905, the Secretariat developed into a fullscale provincial Secretariat. The Chief Commissioner had now an Under Secretary. The Secretariat now consisted of eight branches, divided broadly into two heads, e.g. correspondence and others. The correspondence division consisted of General Branch; Political, Judicial and Military Branch; Revenue Branch; Financial and Municipal Branch. The other division had Issue, Recording, Records, and Library branches.[23] The strength of the Secretariat increased to 99 of which one was Secretary and another Assistant Secretary and a third Under Secretary, 5 Head Assistants, 55 clerks and 35 servants besides a Hospital Assistant. For the garden one Mali was also appointed.[24]

During the period 1905-1912 the Secretariat did not undergo any considerable change. There was, however, an addition to the number of Secretaries, Under Secretaries and Assistant

Secretaries but the internal working and organisation were not changed practically. Each of the Secretaries had under him an office comprising two or more departments each of which was a main division of the public business in the ministerial charge of a Head Assistant.[25] Instead of Superintendent, there was, of course, now a Registrar whose duty was similar to that of Superintendent of the Assam Secretariat.[26]

On the restoration of the Chief Commissionership of Assam in 1912 the Secretariat administration and organization were not changed in anyway. But there was reduction of several positions. Though now two Secretaries were provided to Assam Administration the sanctioned strength of the uncovenanted staff was sixty-six.[27] The bussiness of the correspondence division continued to be subdivided into seven branches e.g. Appointment, Political, Judicial, Revenue, General, Municipal and Education.[28] Each Branch was in the immediate charge of a Head Assistant. The Registrar appointed during the Eastern Bengal and Assam Secretariat continued to control and direct the business of the branches under the Secretaries.[29] The Secretariat staff were subsequently strengthened with the addition of typists and stenographers. The clerks were graded in the Upper and Lower Divisions, though the posts of Head Assistants were retained with a separate scale of pay.[30] There was an overall increase in the strength of the staff. In May 1920, there were 5 Head Assistants, 15 Upper Division and 40 Lower Division clerks, 3 Stenographers, 7 Typists, and 33 Servants.[31]

Administrative Departments

If the Secretariat was the brain of the Local Administration which formulated policies, the different Departments were its hands which executed them. Initially, however, there was no executive Head of a Department, as already noted, to implement the policy of the Local Administration. But for the progress of the province such officers were essential. Therefore, as early as 1876, an Inspector General of Police was appointed.[32] He was also entrusted with the supervision of the departments of Jail, Registration and the office of the Superintendent of Stamps, along with the charge of Commissioner of Excise in the Assam Valley. A Director of Land Records and Agriculture was also appointed in 1882.[33] The Judge of the Assam Valley districts was vested with the powers of a Commissioner of a Division in the Assam Valley in 1880.[34] A separate Judge to relieve the Commissioner of the Assam Valley of his judicial duties was created in 1903.[35] The Medical and Sanitary affairs of the province was initially kept under Deputy Surgeon General of Dacca Circle. But this was inconvenient, it delayed administrative orders and Dacca was too distant a place. Moreover, the province required the service of a separate officer of its own as its problems were particular to itself. Therefore, a Principal Medical Officer was appointed for Assam and he was also made the Sanitary Commissioner of the province.[36] The office of the Inspector of Schools of the province was raised to the status of the Director of Public Instruction commensurate with his increased responsibility and dignity in 1886.[37] The Deputy Conservator of Forest brought under Chief Commissioner was raised to the status of Conservator of Forests.[38] Besides a Commissioner for Excise, an officer for settlement works was also created and a Director for Industries was appointed in 1918.[39]

All these Departmental Officers had their officers in the Secretariat of the Chief Commissioner. A large part of the Government business was transacted by these departmental officers who were constantly in touch with the people through tour and their subordinate agencies.[40] Technically all these departments were separate administrative offices. Located at the Secretariat, they were not under the control of the Secretary to the Chief Commissioner. The Secretary was simply a pipeline through which communications from the Heads of the Departments were sent to the Chief Commissioner and the order of the latter thereon passed on to them. The only exception was the Public Works Department where the Chief Superintending Engineer was also the Secretary of his department to the Chief Commissioner.[41]

Divisional system

The system of Divisional Commissioner was not provided for the Assam Administration in the beginning. It has already been noted that the Headquarters of the province was transferred to Shillong and Shillong was a remote place from many a place of Assam Valley Administrative references to and orders thereon from Shillong took a long time to reach the district officers.

Moreover, with the expansion of administration the Chief Commissioner was burdened too much and it became very difficult for him to scrutinise the references made to him. He, therefore, wanted to get the assistance of a highly responsible officer to dispose locally those business which could be avoided. In 1879, Sir Bayley, therefore, proposed to the Government of India that the Judge of the Assam Valley to be the ex-officio Commissioner of the Assam Valley.[42] High Court objected to the proposal.[43] But Government of India approved the scheme and the Chief Commissioner invested the Judge of the Assam Valley with the powers of a Commissioner of a Division.[44]

The Commissioner had specific statutory powers of his own in addition to those delegated to him by the Local Administration. He exercised direct control over certain branches of district administration. The Chief Commissioner of Assam defined the powers and functions of the Assam Valley Commissioner and his relation with the district officers and the Local government.[45] The Commissioner was the immediate District Educational Officer and the Head of the Educational Department. He was the ex-officio visitor of all the schools in his division. Forest and Immigration Departments had to submit all returns to him.[46] In the administration of Municipality and Forests he was to exercise powers which might be vested in him by the Municipal and Forest Acts in addition to general supervisory powers as the immediate superior of the District Officers.[47]

The Commissioner exercised general supervision over Departments of Stamps, Registration of vital statistics and Sanitation. The Head of the Departments had to consult the Commissioner when necessary in case of doubt and for clarification.[48] The Commissioner was not in more close contact with the people of his division than the Deputy Commissioners of a District and in many cases the residents of a district were scarcely aware of his existence. Nevertheless, a Commissioner acquired invaluable experiences by his supervision over the district administration, he could give valuable help and advise to the provincial Government.

It is quite obvious that the functions of the Commissioner was enormous and it required unremitting zeal and superhuman energy to discharge along with the burden of judgeship the business of the office of Commissioner over of a Division. The territorial jurisdiction was also huge. It was quite natural that initiative and parental care which was expected from a Commissioner of a Local Administration was lacking in the Commissioner of Assam Valley districts. Again the danger of partiality which the Hon'ble High Court of Calcutta had apprehended was latent in the combination of the offices of the Judge and Commissioner. The evil was removed only in 1903 when the offices of the Commissioner and Judge were separated.[49] In the Surma Valley and the Hill District the Chief Commissioner corresponded directly with district officers and no Commissioner was provided till 1905.[50] So we find in 1920 Assam was divided only into two Commissionerships.

The real administration in the province was in the hands of the Deputy Commissioner of the districts. The whole province was divided into 11 districts in 1874. In 1898, another district was created in Lushai Hills.[51] Each district was placed under a Deputy Commissioner who in the eyes of most of its inhabitants was "the Government". A large part of governmental business was done by the Deputy Commissioners.[52] The functions of the Deputy Commissioner changed with the progress of time. He was to collect Revenue, maintain law and order, execute government orders and inspect and co-ordinate the work of the different departments of Government.[53] Gradually, however, with the progress of civilization and increase in the needs of the people, separate departments and separate officers were employed to deal with the different branches of administration. The conception of his office may be summed up thus "the heads of the districts are no longer drudges of many departments and master of none, but in fact the general controlling authority over all departments in each district."[54] The Deputy Commissioner was European covenanted civilian or Military Officer on deputation. Generally, he was in charge of the Headquarters sub-division, but he was allowed one or more assistants.[55]

The Deputy Commissioner of Assam had much more responsibility than their counterparts in other provinces of India. Besides dispensing justice they were required to conduct much important political duties such as the maintenance of peaceful and friendly relation with the hill tribes beyond the administrative frontiers of the province. They had hardly any assistance from any officer for such responsible function. The area of the district under a Deputy Commissioner of Assam averaged 4435 square miles with an average population of 486, 823 persons.[56] As such the administrative area under each seems to be too much when we consider the fastnesses and marshes of the country and undeveloped means of communication.

Each district was divided into a number of sub-divisions. Each sub-division was put under an Assistant Commissioner, usually an European subordinate to the Deputy Commissioner. His duties were similar to that of a Deputy Commissioner within the sub-division. Initially the size of the sub-divisions were bigger. To begin with, there were only 22 sub-divisions in all the 11 districts. The average area of sub-division was 1,971 square miles with a population of 216,365 souls.[57] As administrative works is increased the number of sub-divisions were increased. In 1920 these were 27 sub-divisions in the 12 districts of the province.[58]

The smallest unit of administration in the Assam Valley was originally a Mouza committed to the charge of a Mouzador.[59] He was the representative of the government to the masses in its most visible form. Between 1883 and 1896, the Mouzas were transformed into Tehsils under the charge of superior officers called Tehsildars. But the system of Mouzadars was reintroduced as the Tehsildary system proved unsuccessful.[60] The Mouzadars were Revenue Officers but they assisted the Police Officers in the prevention of crime and detection of criminals. They also desposed of petty disputes of local character. But in every village of Assam Valley there was a recognised village headman who also helped the government officers in Police affairs.[61]

In the hills, the authority of the village headman was more effective in preserving law and order. In every village, in Mikir Hills there was a Me or Mepai presided over by a Gaonbura who decided petty cases and maintained peace in the village.[62] In Mizo Hills there was a Lal who was almost a despot. He collected a revenue from the villagers and saw the observance of customary law.[63] In the Garo Hills, there were Laskars who acted as a kind of Rural Police and Honorary Magistrate for the settlement of petty cases.[64] In the Naga Hills there was a Lambardar in every village who was responsible for the peace and order of the village.[65] In the Khasis and Jaintia Hills there were Siems and Dullois as well as Sardars respectively for the management of the local affairs.[66]

Assam commission

On separation from Bengal, a Chief Commissioner was put in charge of the Local Administration of Assam. His general executive staff consisted of the members of the Assam Commission and the members of provincial and subordinate services. The Government of India transferred eleven Deputy Commissioners, twelve Assistant Commissioners and twenty Extra Assistant Commissioners from the Non-Regulation list of Bengal Government and attached them to Assam Commission.[67] The question of increasing the sanctioned compliment of Assam Commission and the determination of the source from which the substantive vacancies should be filled up were left for future consideration.[68]

Chief Commissioner Keatinge assuming charge of the province explained that the effective Senior Executive Staff should consist of the Chief Commissioner, Inspector General of Police, Jails and Registration (who also held charge of Superintendent of Stamps and Excise in Assam Valley), the Secretary to the Chief Commissioner, the Political Agent to Manipur, the Deputy Commissioner, fifteen Assistant Commissioners and thirty-four Extra Assistant Commissioners of which eight were to be Europeans.[69] But Government of India negativated the proposal for financial reasons.[70]

In 1878, Sir Gorge Bayley again investigated into the requirements of the province and came to the conclusion that 10 Deputy Commissioners, 16 Assistant Commissioners, 26 Extra Assistant Commissioners including 4 European or Eurosians would be required for the daily administration of the province. These excluded the Secretary, Assistant Secretary and Personal Assistant to the Chief Commissioner, Inspector General of Police and Jails and also the requirements of the revenue and settlement works. Moreover, the new sub-divisions that might have been created and Political Officers stationed at Sadiya and North Cachar Hills were also excluded from this estimate. But the sanctioned strength of the Commission was eleven Deputy Commissioners, twenty Assistant Commissioners and two probationers. The minimum requirement of the province was eleven Deputy Commissioners and twenty-three Assistant Commissioners and three probationers.[71] According to Government of India formula, the minimum requirement for the daily administration of the province ought to have been eleven Deputy Commissioners, eighteen Assistant Commissioners, three European Extra Assistant Commissioners and three Assistant Commissioners for special appointments. To this should be added reserved for filling leave vacancies and trainee officers.[72] But in July 1878, the Commission consisted of 11 Deputy Commissioners, 19 Assistant Commissioners of which 16 were military personnel on deputation in civil duty and 14 were civilians deputed from Bengal. Besides there were 25 Extra Assistant Commissioners. But the Staff sanctioned for the Commission did not provide for filling vacancies on leave, deputation and trainee officers.[73]

The strength of the Assam Commission in 1881 was 13 Deputy Commissioners, 19 Assistant Commissioners of which 2 Deputy Commissioners were on furlough and of 19 Assistant Commissioners of which 4 were on furlough, one was transferred to North-Western Province and one was on Census duty. There were also four Superintendents. Of total 36 officres 28 were on district duty and 8 were on leave. But 27 officers were absolutely necessary to run the administration excluding the Inspector General of Police and Secretary to the Chief Commissioner.[74] Sir Elliot therefore requested for 2 officers from Bengal or Central Province or Punjab in addition to 2 young probationer who were expected to join very soon. But even in 1888, we find the finance refusing to recognise 20.58 plus 27.39 furlough reserve.[75]

On reorganization in 1900 the strength of the Assam Commission was reduced from 47 to 39, 6 posts being added to Provincial Civil Service.[76] But the actual number of Officers appointed were 41 of which 29 were civilians and 12 were military and uncovenanted officers.[77]

During the period of 1905 to 1912 only two members were added to the Commission rank for Assam. One of them was the Commissioner for Surma Valley and Hill district and the second was the Additional Magistrate for Sylhet. On restoration of the Chief Commissionership the two posts were retained and another Secretary to the Chief Commissioner was provided with an Under Secretary of the rank of Assistant Commissioner. There were besides a Commissioner of Excise and a Settlement Officer.[78] But a significant risk took place in the ranks of Provincial Civil Services. There were 60 Extra Assistant Commissioners and 61 Sub-Deputy Collectors.[79]

Thus the members of the Assam Commission in 1912 was 48 though only 45 were employed in actual administration. The rest was kept as reserve for leave and deputation for Government of India service. Of these posts 22 including the Chief Commissioner were superior posts and the rest were inferior.

On the constitution of a Province in 1922, the strength of the Commission was raised to 51, 47 for administration of the province and 2 were kept for deputation and 2 for Government of India Services. But the strength of the Assam Civil Service was raised to 84 Extra Assistant Commissioners and of the Subordinate Service to 84 Sub-Deputy Collectors.

Recruitment and number

The system by which vacancies in Assam Commission was filled up was to borrow from Bengal the Junior Civilians for term of 5 years after which they had the option to revert to their cadre post in Bengal. But for administrative necessity the officers might be retained for a longer period than five years. Usually a portion of the vacancy was filled up by Military Officers deputed on civil duty.[80] The system proved very inexpedient. The officers after gaining experience often reverted to their positions in Bengal. So the administration lost the fruits of their experience and service. Again Army officers often showed a lack of tact and enterprise, the usual qualities of a Civil Officer.[81]

The possibility of creating a separate cadre of Assam Commission was mooted several times. But it was found impossible to create a separate cadre for Assam consisting of so small a number of officers. The scope for promotion was so meagre that almost there was no opening to promising officers. Therefore, the service had very little attraction for talented people.[82] Moreover, the pay of the officers was also comparatively low. An officer of similar rank in other provinces, even in Bengal, was drawing more salary than his counterpart in

Assam. Finally, the climate and conditions of the province had very little attraction for the European Officers.[83] Yet Assam required a larger proportion of European officers for obvious reasons. The frontier relation of the administration, the tea gardens which were regulated under modern system of labour enactments and inspected by District Officers, a larger European population in the province—all required the care and discretion which the British did not like to be entrusted to the native officers.[84] Therefore the manning of the vacancies in the Assam Commission remained a problem.

REFERENCES

1. Prasad, B. : The Origins of Provincial Autonomy, p. 1.
2. Ibid., p. 3.
3. Ibid., p. 9.
4. Ilbert Courtney : The Government of India, p. 93.
5. Prasad, B. : The Origins of Provincial Autonomy, p. 47.
6. Ibid., p. 12.
7. PGIHPUB No. 517 of October, 1873.
8. Ibid., No. 527 of October, 1873.
9. Ibid.
10. Ibid., No. 533 of October, 1873.
11. Ibid., No. 533 of October, 1873.
12. Ibid., No. 181-183 of December 1874.
13. Ibid.
14. RAA 1874-76, part IIA, para 137-138.
15. Old Record File No. 93-189 B.G.
16. Ibid.
17. RAA, 1874-76, Part IIB, para 4.
18. Rules of Business in the Assam Secretariat, Rule 131.
19. Ibid., Rule 118.
20. PGIHEST Nos. 138-140 of December, 1874.
21. File No. 620/G. 1874 (Assam State Archives).
22. PGIHEST No. 111-113 of June, 1874.
23. Rules of Business in the Assam Secretariat, Rule 1.
24. PGFIN No. 273-76 of May 1905.
25. Provisional Rules of Business, Eastern Bengal and Assam Secretariat Rule 1.
26. Ibid., Rule 167.
27. List of Business in the Assam Secretariat, January, 1915.
28. Ibid.
29. Ibid.
30. PGAGD Nos. 220-225 of November, 1920.

31. Ibid.
32. PGIHEST Nos. 35-36 of October, 1876.
33. RAA 1881-82, part IIB, para 171.
34. Ibid., para 1.
35. PGIHEST Nos. 19-22 of February, 1902.
36. RAA 1892-93, part IIB, para 116.
37. PGAGD No. 1 of February, 1889.
38. RAA 1892-93, part IIB, para 116.
39. RAA 1920-21, part II, para 113.
40. Report of the Indian Statutory Commission Vol. I, para 312.
41. RAA 1874-76, part IIA, para 140.
42. PGIHEST No. 19-22 of February, 1902.
43. Ibid.
44. Ibid.
45. Manual of Executive Rules and Orders in Force in Assam, p. 85.
46. Ibid.
47. Ibid., p. 86.
48. Ibid.
49. PGIHEST No. 19-22 of February, 1902.
50. REABA 1905-06, part II, para 118.
51. RAA 1874-76, part IIA, para 270.
52. RAA 1821-22, part II, para 145. The Officer-in-charge of Lushai Hills was a Superintendent he was not styled Deputy Commissioner.
53. Imperial Gazatteer Vol. IV, p. 49
54. Report of the Indian Statutory Commission, Vol. I, para 289.
55. RAA 1874-76 part IIA, para 125.
56. Imperial Gazatteer, Vol. VI, p. 82.
57. Ibid.
58. RAA 1921-22, part II, para 145.
59. RAA 1874-76, part IIA, para 126.
60. Imperial Gazatteer, Vol. VI, p. 82.
61. Ibid., p. 100.
62. Rao, V. Venkata : Hundred Years of Local Self-Government, p. 103.
63. Ibid.
64. Ibid., p. 104.
65. Ibid., p. 105.
66. Imperial Gazatteer, Vol. VI, p. 83.
67. PGIHEST No. 104 of June, 1874.
68. Ibid.
69. PGA No. 2 of 4 September, 1878, para 2.
70. Ibid.
71. Ibid., para 4.
72. PGA No. 2 of October, 1878, para 8.
73. Ibid.
74. PGA No. 21 of October, 1881.
75. Ibid.
76. PGA No. 28 March, 1904.

77. Ibid.
78. PGA No. 8 of August, 1912.
79. Ibid.
80. PGA No. 5 of July 1978.
81. Ibid.
82. PGIHEST No. 168 of March, 1898.
83. Ibid.
84. PGA No. 18 of April, 1888.

4

HEAD OF THE PROVINCE CHIEF COMMISSIONER

THE HEAD of the province that is, the Chief Commissioner was the pivot of the provincial Government. He was not only a delegate of the Governor-General-in-Council but also the actual ruler of the territories of his province. He was the keystone of the structure of the administrative machinery of the province. He was commissioned to be the custodian of the provincial Government and the representative of the sovereign masters. As such he was not only the first dignitary of the province but also the Chief Executive of it. And subject to the authority of the Supreme Government he was the final authority of the Local Administration. With him was also entrusted the general well-being of the province as well as its inhabitants.

The immediate task of the British, in 1826 after the conclusion of peace by the Treaty of Yandabu was to provide a well knit administrative set-up for Assam as the Ahom Administrative system collapsed completely during the Burmese invasion. Mr. David Scott and Col. Richards were entrusted with the management of the territories conquered in Assam. In April, 1826, a kind of dyarchy was brought into existence.[1] Mr. David Scott was appointed Political Agent. He was entrusted with the management of the newly acquired tract while Col. Richards was entrusted with the administration of civil and criminal justice in addition to the Police Establishment at Gauhati. Mr. Scott was held responsible for the collection of revenues. Capt. Davidson was appointed his Assistant. But the Political Agent was forbidden from interfering with matters of purely military nature though he should give more cordial and zealous support to the Officer Commanding on all questions of general interest.[2] In 1828 Martial law was withdrawn from Assam and the post of Junior Commissioner was abolished. Assam was placed under a Commissioner who was also the Political Agent to the Governor-General-in-Council.[3]

The office of the Commissioner was created in 1807.[4] The Commissioner was at first a Revenue Officer responsible for the collection of Revenue. But the Regulation I of 1829 enlarged the powers and functions of the Commissioners.[5] Appointed by the Board of Revenue, the Commissioner was to supervise the administration of his circle. He was supposed to be accessible to the people and was to exercise, until otherwise specially provided for by law, the duties, powers and authority vested in the Board of Revenue and the Court of Wards. In the exercise of powers he was subject to the control and direction of Sadar Board of Revenue and guided in his proceedings by the orders of the Government.[6] He was also vested with both civil and criminal powers. He was authorised to exercise full powers of a Circuit Judge. He was to hold half yearly sessions of goal deliveries. Regulation 7 of 1831 designated the Commissioner as a Sessions Judge and authorised him to try cases committed by the Magistrates.[7] Further, he was also the Superintendent of Police. The Commissioner of Assam as Political Agent, was entrusted with the general management and control of all Political transactions and negotiations that were to be conducted with tribal chiefs inhabiting the hills and plains of Assam.[8]

But the peculiar circumstances of Assam necessitated the creation of a separate province for Assam and the care and powers of an exclusive Chief Executive for it. Therefore, Assam was made a separate province in 1874 and was placed under a Chief Commissioner.[9]

The form of administration under a Chief Commissioner was more personal than formal. Where newly acquired territories required a Government, a Chief Commissionership provided a unique system.[10] Generally such a territory was governed by a ruder and simpler fashion by an executive composed partly of civilians and partly of soldiers. The executive would respect and venerate all that was good in the native institutions and in the local usages of the country.[11] The Chief of the Administration in such a province would take quick action depending upon the exigencies of any situation.[12] The Secretary of State wrote to the Governor-General-in-Council in connection with the formation of the Chief Commissionership "I cannot doubt that, when strength and directness of power are required in any subordinate administration, it is best to place that administration immediately under the Supreme Government, so that it may, as directly as possible, enjoy the support and carry the authority, of the Governor-General-in-Council. Assam and the eastern districts seem to be eminently a case requiring such an administration."[13]

The title of the Chief Commissioner was first used in 1853 when Mr. John Lawrence of Punjab was appointed Head of the Executive Government in substitution of the former Board of administrators under a President.[14] It was to distinguish the Head of the Administration from the Financial and Judicial Commissioners who were also appointed at the same time.[15] In early times the title given to such a delegate of administrative functions was, of course, a Commissioner, as in the case of Mr. Mounstuart Elphinstone when appointed to administer the territories in the Deccan conquered from the Peshwas in 1818.[16] Later on the Act of 1854 was passed to set-up a Chief Commissionership. The Act provided that the Governor-General-in-Council, with the sanction of the Board of Control and the Court of Directors may, by proclamation, take under his immediate authority and management any territory and provide for its administration.[17] But the title of the Chief Commissioner was not recognised by any act of Parliament, and as such the territories committed to the charge of a Chief Commissioner is theoritically under the immediate authority and management of the Governor-General-in-Council. Therefore, in official terminology, Chief Commissionership was regarded as a Local Administration rather than a Local Government.[10]

The common designation of the Chief Executive of Local Government in India was Governor or Lt. Governor upto 1854 or a Chief Commissioner thereafter. The Governors of the three Presidency Provinces of Calcutta, Bombay and Madras were appointed by the Crown in England on the recommendation of the Secretary of State for India.[19] These posts were reserved for talented and ambitious members of British aristocracy. Usually persons of public life in Britain, holding a prominent place in the Party in powers and often possessing some amount of parliamentary experience were preferred for these posts.[20] But the Governors of all other provinces were appointed on recommendation of the Viceroy. Senior members of Indian Civil Service with a record of long administration experience in various départments were considered for these posts.[21] A young civilian starting his career at the lowest rung of the bureaucratic ladder of administration could hope to rise through successive stages by a brilliant official record of industry, tact and success in the performance of their duties to the post of the head of a province. Attractive salary, immense powers and prime status of the office induced the Englishmen to join the Indian Civil Service.[22]

The Chief Commissioner was appointed by the Governor-General-in-Council from amongst the senior covenanted or civil servants of the Company who had distinguished themselves in administration, for a term of five years.[23] They were, usually men of vast experience in different fields of Indian Administration. Though there was no statutory term for the office of the Chief Commissioners or their pay, Government of India clarified the doubt in this respect by an order issued to the Chief Commissioner of Assam.[24] It stated that Chief Commissioner should continue in office for five years including the period of officiating term preceding the confirmation in the post. The pay was fixed at Rs. 4,666-10-8 per month plus a sumptuary allowance of Rs. 500/- per month.[25]

As for the duties of the head of the Province the Act of 1833 provided that the executive Government of each presidency would be administered by a Governor-in-Council. He would not make laws or sanction new expenditure. But otherwise the whole administration of the province was assigned to him.[26] The Act of 1854 empowered the Governor-General to declare and limit the extent of authority of the Lieutenant Governor or Chief Commissioner when the latter posts were envisaged.[27] But no such definition was ever given and the chief of the provinces carried on the administration of their provinces under the eye of the Supreme Government.[28] But naturally the superintendence of the latter was incomplete. In earlier days due to lack of swift communication all executive Government was left at the discretion of the Local Head of the Administration. It was always convenient for the Supreme Government to delegate by law the execution of the details of administration to the Local Government.[29] The functions which these Governments exercised were very comprehensive and included almost everything which affected the happiness of the people and the stability of the provincial Government.[30]

Government under a chief commissioner

The Chief Commissioner's Administration was Local Government, and though the Governor-General did not divest himself of any of his inherent powers, the Chief Commissioner was according to Indian Law, the person authorisedto administer executive Government.[31] A Chief Commissioner exercised powers and functions similar to that of a Governor of a Province. For example, all the powers of the Lt. Governor of Bengal so far as Assam was concerned were taken over by the Governor-General-in-Council and delegated to the Chief Commissioner of Assam without any reservation.* Moreover, the powers of the Board of Revenue over Assam were also taken over from it and vested in the Chief Commissioner who was thus made the repository of more powers than the Lt. Governor of Bengal. Further with the creation of the Legislative Council in Assam in 1912, all vestiges of difference between a Governor's province and the Chief Commissioner's administration of Assam practically disappeared.[32]

Functions of the chief commissioner

The functions of Government fall mainly under three heads—Legislative, Executive and Judicial. The Chief Commissioner being the head of the Province who represented the Government of India had also three-fold functions. In Legislation, the Chief Commissioner under Section 1 of the Act XXXIII, Q. Vict. Cap-2 (An Act to make better provisions for making laws and Regulations for certain parts of India and for certain other purposes there to had power to propose to the Governor-General-in-Council, drafts of any Regulation, together with the

*The powers delegated to the Chief Commissioner of Assam in 1874-76 are given in the appendix to this Chapter.

reasons for proposing the same, for the peace and good Government of territories under his administration.[33] Such drafts when approved by the Governor-General-in-Council and after they had received Governor-General's assent were published in the Gazettes of India and Assam and thereupon had the force of law in the Province.[34] This was made applicable to the districts of Kamrup, Darrang, Nowgong, Sibsagar, Lakhimpur, Garo Hills, Khasi and Jaintia Hills, Naga Hills, and Cachar from 1 January, 1873 Sylhet from 1 August, 1874 and Goalpara from 15 December, 1873, after a resolution to that effect was passed by the Secretary of State for Indian in Council.[35]

Again, the Chief Commissioner of the Act, XIV of 1874 (Scheduled District Act) could extend to the province, with the previous sanction of the Governor-General-in-Council, any measure passed by the other local legislators of British India which appeared to him necessary for his province, by notification in the Gazettes of India and Assam.[36] Section 6, clause C, the Chief Commissioner was empowered to define by what authority and jurisdiction, powers or duties incident to the operation of any enactment for the time being in force in a Scheduled district would be exercised and performed.[37]

During 1905-1911 when Assam became a part of the new province of Eastern Bengal and Assam, the provisions of the Indian Councils Act, 1861 was extended to it.[38] The Lt. Governor of the province was authorised to nominate fifteen Councillors to the provincial Council with the approval of the Governor General-in-Council.[39] So also the Lt. Governor was to prepare the rules of procedure of the Council.[40] The Act provided that the Lt. Governor was to be the President of the Council and he had to notify the date, time and place of meeting of the Council.[41] He was also competent to suspend any rule or rules for sufficient reason or prorogue or suspend the meetings of the Council.[42] The bills passed by the Council had to be assented to by the Lt. Governor, of course, the bills had to be submitted to the Governor-General-in-Council for approval.[43] The Indian Councils Act 1909 did not materially change the powers and functions of the Chief of the State, if merely enhanced the non-official membership of the Council and extend their tenure of office from 2 to 3 years.[44]

On the restoration of the Chief Commissionership in 1912, the Secretary of State agreed to the establishment of a Legislative Council for Assam.[45] The Governor-General-in-Council, therefore, extended the provisions of Indian Councils Act, 1861 to 1909 on 14 November, 1912 to Assam.[46] The rules in force for the conduct of business of the Legislative Council of the defunct province of Eastern Bengal and Assam, except in details was adopted for the new Council.[47] The Chief Commissioner was the president of the Council. He fixed the date, time and place of meeting of the Council. He prepared the order of business of the Council and could prorogue, suspend or adjourn its meetings. Bills, passed by the Council, required his assent before it could be sent for the approval of the Governor-General-in-Council.[48]

Thus the Chief of the State was relieved much of the Legislative business by the creation of the Council. But he continued to exercise, section 1 of the Act XXXIII, Q. Vict. Cap-3 for the good Government of the Frontier Tracts and the Hill Districts.[49] And Section 5 of Act XIV of 1874.[50] Indeed centralisation of legislative authority in province like Assam inhabited by sundry backward tribes was wellneigh impossible. Here the responsibility of the Chief Commissioner did not diminish.

Judicial

The judicial functions of the Chief Commissioner was relieved by retaining the jurisdiction of the High Court of Calcutta over the plains districts of the Assam Valley and Sylhet and Cachar.[51] But over the hill areas of the frontier and the districts of Garo, Naga, Lushai and North Cachar, the High Court had no jurisdiction except over the European British subjects. The Chief Commissioner was the Highest Court of Appeal for them.[52] Since 1905, the Chief of the province also enjoyed the power to grant reprieves in cases in which sentences of death had been passed in permanently settled portion of the province.[53]

Executive

The Chief Commissioner was the representative of the Governor-General-in-Council in the province and as such the Chief

Executive. All executive authority vested in him and the administration was carried in his name. The Chief Commissioner had to inspect all the branches of administration personally and attend to all enquiries and references.[54] He was in a sense a Commissioner writ large.

The general executive staff of the province consisted of the member of the Assam Commission and the members of the provincial and subordinate executive services.[55] In 1874, there was no Departmental Head to aid and advise the Chief Commissioner or any Commissioner between the district and the provincial Government.[56] He was, however, given a Secretary and an Assistant Secretary to help him in the discharge of duties.[57]

In July, 1875 the Chief Commissioner had issued a circular to all the Deputy Commissioners that as there was no Comissioners or Inspector General of Police or any other Departmental Officers to aid and advise the Chief Commissioner—he would expect them to be more responsible in their supervision and inspection works.[58] The Deputy Commissioners should inspect all the departments of district administration and in case of any doubt they should make reference to the Chief Commissioner.[59]

But with the development of the province as well as regularisation of the administrative procedure it was difficult for the Chief Commissioner to supervise all the aspects of the provincial Government all by himself. As already noted as early as 1876 an Inspector General of Police was appointed to relieve him of his police responsibilities. That officer was also entrusted with the supervision of the departments of Jail, Registration and Stamps along with the responsibilities of the Excise branch in the Assam Valley.[60] A Director of Land Records and Agriculture was appointed in 1882 for the efficient administration of Land Revenue and Settlement works. The Judicial Commissioner of Assam Valley districts was vested with the powers of a Commissioner of a Division in the Assam valley districts. In 1903, the Secretary of State sanctioned a Commissioner, a separate judge for Assam Valley and he relieved of his judicial works. The Department of Education entrusted originally to an Inspector was made over to a more responsible officer of Director of Public Instruction in 1886. The Medical and Sanitary affairs looked after by the

Deputy-Surgeon General of Dacca Circle was taken over by a Principal Medical Officer of Assam. Even the Forests had to be entrustedto a Conservator of Forests.[61]

Thus the Chief Commissioner was assisted and aided gradually by a number of officers who were responsible for the efficient administration of the Departments committed to their charges. A large amount of Government business including communication with the general public was done through them.[62] These Departments were located in the Secretariat of the Chief Commissioner. The Secretary received communication on behalf of the Chief Commissioner from these Heads of the Departments.[63]

When Assam was amalgamated with Eastern Bengal, the Head of the province was made Lt. Governor. The Chief of the provincial administration occupied now a significant position. He administered an extensive territory, commanded a larger staff, wielded more patronage and power and was vested with more responsibility.[64] His responsibility was not shared by any Executive Council.[65] Subject to the control of the Government of India his authority was complete and orders final. All these factors enhanced his prestige and position. He could not, however, impose any tax or charge the existing revenue management.[66]

In 1912, when Assam was again placed under a Chief Commissioner, the executive powers and functions of the province increased considerably. Practically he exercised the powers and functions of a Governor of a province.* His Secretariat now consisted of three Secretaries, three Under-Secretaries and eight Heads of departments. All the subjects were directly under his control.[67]

In retrospect it seems that in the possession and exercise of powers over the provincial administration in their charge, all the Chiefs of the Provinces of British India were almost absolutely equal.[68] Their control over the administrative machinery of the province, the official status and privileges which they enjoyed within their respective jurisdictions were

*On separation from Eastern Bengal, the Local Government of Assam was now the Chief Commissioner's Administration and he continued to exercise all the powers and perform all the functions of the Lt. Governor of the defunct province of Eastern Bengal and Assam.

also identical although the factors which establish the pre-eminence of the Heads of the province in all aspects of the provincial life were not similar in every province.[69] But inspite of this equality in prestige and power, there was a kind of gradation in the office of the Chief of the province. The size of the province, their population and resources made some provinces important and other less considerable.[70] These were reflected in the salaries and allowances that were paid to these Chiefs of the Provinces.

Be that as it may, Chief Commissioner was the Head of the Local Government as a delegate of the Governor-General-in-Council. He was responsible for the good Government of the province. It was his duty to initiate any measure that would promote the welfare of the people and ensure peace and security to the Empire. He, therefore, called for all information and suggestions for administrative purpose from his officers. It was also essential for him to communicate to the Government of India any information regarding matters of political or administrative importance or events which excited public interest. The matters which the Government of India particularly desired to receive earliest possible information were which involved serious breach of public peace, all collisions between Europeans of all classes and Indians, outrages which had a political import, calamities such as floods or earthquakes which had administrative and political importance.[71] The cumulative effect of discharge of all these powers and functions, normal and special, ordinary and extraordinary legislative, executive and judicial, made the position of the Chief Commissioner formidable. And when the Chief Commissionership was converted into a Governor's Province there was merely a change in status and not in powers, of the Head of the province.

REFERENCE

1. Lahiri, R. M.: The Annexation of Assam, p. 15.
2. Lahiri, R.M: The Annexation of Assam, p. 15.
3. Barpuzari, H.K.: Assam in the Days of the Company, p. 35.
4. Misra, B.B.: The Central Administration of the East India Company, p. 142.
5. Ibid., p. 149.

6. Misra, B.B.: The Central Administration of the East India Company, p. 151.
7. Ibid., p. 151.
8. Lahiri, R.M.: The Annexation of Assam, p. 15.
9. RAA 1874-76, part IIA, para 123.
10. Kaye : The Administration of the East India Company, p. 433.
11. Ibid.
12. Ibid.
13. PGIHPUB No. 517 of October, 1873.
14. Imperial Gazatteer, Vol. IV, p. 32.
15. Ibid.
16. Ibid.
17. Ilbert, Courtney : The Government of India, p. 93.
18. Report on Indian Constitutional Reforms, para 42.
19. Palande, M. R. : Indian Administration, p. 275.
20. Ibid.
21. Ibid.
22. Ibid., p. 276.
23. Ilbert: The Government of India, p. 142.
24. PGA No. 5 of August 1913.
25. Ibid.
26. Prasad, B.: The Origins of Provincial Autonomy, p. 22.
27. Section 4 of Government of India Act, 1854.
28. Prasad, B.: The Origins of Provincial Autonomy, p. 23.
29. Ibid.
30. Ibid.
31. Imperial Gazatteer, Vol. IV, p. 53.
32. Report on Indian Constitutional Reforms, para 42.
33. RAA 1874-76, part IIA, para 143.
34. Ibid.
35. Ibid., para 144.
36. RAA 1893-94, part II, para 2.
37. RAA 1880-81, part IIB, para 2.
38. RAA 1911-12, part II, para 218.
39. Ibid.
40. PGIHPUB Nos. 218-219 of February, 1907.
41. Ibid.
42. Ibid., Nos. 65-66 of February, 1906.
43. Ibid.
44. RAA 1911-12, part II, para 218.
45. PGIHPUB Nos. 91-92 of July, 1912.
46. RAA 1911-12, part II, para 219.
47. PGIHPUB Nos. 155-156 of November, 1912.
48. PGIHPUB No. 155 of November, 1912.
49. RAA 1911-12, part II, para 224.
50. Ibid., para 222.
51. RAA 1874-76, part IIB, para 124.
52. Ibid.

53. Ibid.
54. PGIHPUB No. 181 of December, 1874.
55. Imperial Gazetteer Vol. VI, p. 82.
56. PGIHPUB No. 181 of December, 1874.
57. RAA 1874-76, part IIB, para 124.
58. PGA No. 1 of July, 1875.
59. Ibid.
60. Supra p. 48.
61. Ibid., p. 49.
62. Report of the Indian Statutory Commission Vol. I, para 312.
63. Ibid.
64. RAEBA 1905-06, part II, para 124.
65. Ibid.
66. Ibid.
67. RAA 1912-13, part II, para 105.
68. Palande, M.R.: Indian Administration, p. 274.
69. Ibid., p. 275.
70. Ibid.
71. Manual of Executive Rules and Orders in force in Assam Rule 15A.

APPENDIX

The following powers were exercised by the Lt. Governor of Bengal in Assam and taken over by the Governor-General-in-Council from the former and were subsequently delegated to the Chief Commissioner of Assam in the years 1874-76.*

1. The powers of an Inspector-General of Police under Act of 1861 and VII (B.C.) of 1869.
2. The powers of a Local Government under Act XXII of 1864 (Cantonments).
3. The powers of a Local Government under Act VII of 1865 (Forest).
4. The powers of a Local Government under Section 22, Act CCCI of 1860 (Arms and Ammunition).
5. The powers of Local Government under Section 624, Act XX of 1865 (Pleaders).
6. The powers of Local Government under Section 16, 18, 29, 35, 37, Act VI of 1871 (Civil Courts Bengal).
7. The powers of the Board of Revenue, Lower Provinces, under Act XXI of 1856 (Excise).
8. The powers of a Local Government under Section 2, 5, Act II (B.C.) of 1867 (Gambling).
9. The powers which were exercised by the Lt. Governor of Bengal under the following sections and classes of Act VII (B.C.) of 1873 (Labour District Immigration), namely, Section 4, classes 2, 10, 11, 12 and 13, Sections 37, 98, 104, 114 and 119.
10. The powers heretofore vested in, or exercisable by the Board Revenue of the Lower Provinces, under all the rules made before the 2nd February, 1874, under which waste land grants were held in the Province of Assam.
11. The powers which, under, or by virtue of Act IV (B.C.) of 1870 (an act to consolidate and amend the law relating the court of wards within the provinces under the control of the Lt. Governor of Bengal) were heretofore vested in,

RAA 1874-76, part IIB, para 3.

or exerciseable by the Board of Revenue of the Lower province.

12. The powers vested in the Board of Revenue of the Lower Province under Act XX of 1865 (an Act to amend the law relating to pleaders and mukhtears).
13. The power to appoint to any revenue jurisdiction a Deputy Collector, with the powers and duties referred to in Bengal Regulation IX of 1833, Sections 17, 18 and 20 to 24, both inclusive.
14. The powers under the Rules for the sale of waste land, published in part 1 of the Calcutta Gazette of the 4th February, 1874
15. The powers which were exercised by the Lt. Governor of Bengal under Act III (B.C.) of 1864 (The District Municipal Improvement Act) as amended by Bengal Act VII of 1867, II of 1868, and II of 1873.
16. The power of a Local Government under Sections 26 and 49 of Act XI of 1859 (the Revenue sale Law).
17. The powers of the Bengal Board of Revenue, Lowers Province under Sections 3, 4, 19, 26 and 49 of Act XI of 1859 (the Revenue Sale Law).
18. The powers which were vested in, or exercisable by, the Lt. Governor of Bengal, under Sections 2, 5, 11, 21, 25, 37, 41 and 92 of Act VI (B.C.) of 1868 (an Act to provide for the better regulation of Police in Towns, and for the conservancy and improvement thereof).
19. The powers of a local government under Sections 5 and 25 of Act VII (B.C.) of 1868 (an act for the recovery of arrears of land revenue).
20. The powers of a local government under Sections 1, 2, 35, 41, 49, 50, 51, 62, 70, 75, 76, 78 79, 83 and 97 of Act X (B.C.) of 1871 (the District Road Law Act).
21. The powers of the Board of Revenue, Lower Province, under Section 14 of Act VIII (B.C.) of 1865 (an act to amend the law for the sale of such under tenures as by the title deeds or establishes usage of the country are transferable by the sale or otherwise, for the recovery of arrears of rent due in respect thereof).
22. The powers which are exercisable by the Government of Bengal under Section 2, 3 and 11 of Act VIII (B.C.) of

1862 (an act to improve the system of Zaminderi daks in the provinces subject to the Government of Bengal).

23. The power of an Inspector General of Jails under Act XXVI of 1870 (Judicial).
24. All the powers in respect to settlements of the land Revenue of the Lower Provinces.
25. All the powers having reference to the partition of estates, which were vested in, or exercisable by the Board of Revenue of the Lower Provinces under Regulation XIX of 1814, and Acts XX of 1836 and XI of 1838.
26. The powers vested in, or exercised by, the Lt. Governor of Bengal under Sections 2, 4, 6, 7, 8 and 9 of Regulation I of 1873 (now called act V of 1873)—Bengal Eastern Frontier Regulation, 1873.
27. The powers of specially appointing officers to exercise the powers of a Magistrate of Police under Act XIII of 1859 (an act to provide for the punishment of breaches of contract by artificers, workmen and labourers).
28. All powers which were vested in the Lt. Governor of Bengal by the direct operation of any act of the Governor-General-in-Council, which also countered the same powers on the Chief Commissioners of Oudh the Central Provinces and British Burma.

5

ADMINISTRATION OF LAND REVENUE

AFTER the assumption of Dewani, the British did not change immediately either the principle or the se-tup of the indigenous revenue organisation of the Bengal Subah and it was only after they had acquired sufficient knowledge that they introduced changes gradually. In the case of Assam also Mr. David Scott, tried to use the indigenous machinery till a better system could be divised.[1]

During the Ahom rule the king was the absolute owner of land. Each subject was allotted land under certain conditions.[2] Generally the whole population with the exception of men of rank and their slaves was divided on the basis of occupation into a number of units called "Khel" which comprised 1,000 to 5,000 persons. The 'Khel' was subdivided again into a number of sub-unit, called "Got" consisting of four and later three persons called "Pyke". Each "Pyke" was bound to serve the King either as a private or public servant personally for a term of the year during which other members of the 'Got' cultivated his land. For his service the Pyke was granted two puras* of ropit land termed as 'guamati'. In addition he was granted a piece of land for garden and house for which he was to pay a Poll tax or House tax or Health tax.[3] If a 'Pyke' cultivated land in excess of two puras, he had to pay one rupee per pura as revenue.[4] Thus much of the revenue was received in service. But the 'Khel' of non-cultivating people paid tax in cash. Thus

*Two Puras—$2\frac{2}{3}$ acres. Please see Imperial Gazetteer, Vol. VI, p. 89.

the Braziers and the Gold-washers had to pay a tax of rupees 5, Oil Pressers Rs. 3, Fishermen Rs. 2.[5] Farming of markets and fisheries and custom posts also yielded some revenue.[6] Finally the vassals of the King paid tribute and people gave presents to the king.

Mr. David Scott abolished the system of personal service and instead introduced a tax of Rs. 3 per Pyke for his home stead, garden and rice land.[7] In 1832 the system was changed. Each district was divided into Mahals which were settled upto 1835 annually after assessment.[8] The revenue was collected through commissioned agents called Chaudhuries, Mouzadars and Kakoties.[9] This system continued till 1836 when the plan for settlement of a group of villages called Mouza form a short term with contractors called Chaudhuries or Mouzadars was introduced.[10] But in 1854 the system of annual settlement was reverted to.[11] The lands however were divided into three classes and rents for the different classes were also different. But the question of raising the assessment of land and also giving the cultivators a permanent, heritable and transferable right in their land was discussed during the period between 1861 and 1867.[12]

The Lt. Governor of Bengal in consultation with the Board of Revenue came to conclusion that after local enquires and field measurement settlement was to be effected on the following principles.[13]

(a) The term of settlement was to be ten years but the Deputy Commissioner as his discretion could make it for fifteen years as well.

(b) Settlement was to be made with the occupant cultivators.

(c) Rates of assessment was to be fixed for the period of settelement but could be altered after the period was over.

(d) Permanent holdings were to be heritable and transferable on condition that transfer would be registered.

(e) Lands brought under cultivation during the currency of a settlement was to be assessed on actual measurement year by year, but a heritable and transferable title was not to be conferred on the cultivators in respect of such land until the next settlement, and then only if found in possession.

(f) Revenue was to be collected by Mouzadars who were to be allowed no property right in the land but were to be remunerated by a commission on the revenue they collect.

The Commissioner of Assam accordingly drew up a set of rules based on the above principles which came into force in 1870.[14] Under these rules the whole of Assam was divided into Mouzas or circles under Mouzadars, each Mouza again being sub-divided into a number of groups of villages containing not less than 2,000 houses under Mandals who were the assistants of the Mouzadars.[15] The Mouzadar was required to execute an agreement with the Government for the collection of revenue for which he was given a commission but he had no interest in land. The Mouzadar was to take measurement of the lands under him with a 30 feet long chain and record his measurement in a field register (Chitha) from which an abstract (Khatian) and a revenue roll (Jamabandi) were to be prepared.[16] All cultivated lands were divided into two classes—"fixed cultivation and "fluctuating cultivation"[17] The former included rupit and homestead lands, while the later included all high paddy lands and lands where mustard seeds and pulses could be grown. On the basis of mouzadars measurement regular and supplimentary settlements were made and the settlement of each cultivator's holding was completed by the issue of a Patta to him or lease, and taking from him a Kabuliyat or acceptance, in prescribed form[18]

Under the rules of 1870 the "fixed cultivation" land were settled more or less permanently and were known as "settled assessments", it being assumed that they would rarely be called for revision.[19] The "fluctuating cultivation" lands were settled for one year only at a time, terminating with the financial year.[20] In the case of "settled assessment", the cultivator was allowed the option of taking a lease for any period not exceeding ten years during which assessment could not be changed.[21] These holdings were declared to be heritable and transferable subject to their being registered.[22] The leasee was allowed the option to relinquish the holding at three months notice as was the case with annual leases.[23] In the case of "fluctuating cultivation" lands, the rules allowed only annual lease and the government could take away such land if required for public purpose without giving any compensation, compensation being allowed for standing crops or houses only.[24]

The settlement rules of 1870 were first public declaration of the rights in land possessed by the cultivators of the soil. These remained in force till 1887 when Land and Revenue Regulation superceded them.[25] The Land and Revenue Regulation of 1886 did not change the principles of the settelment rules of 1870. Rather it plugged the loopholes and elaborated the existing rules to meet changing requirements. Subsequently in 1883 after cadastral survey decennial settlement rules were passed. Under these rules settlements were to be made only of lands which were to be held permanently.[26]

Resettlement of Assam proper was again made for ten years in 1893.[27] The main principle on which the reassessment and resettlement were made was that of recognising the demand for land as the factor determining its value, and therefore its rate.[28] A provisional classification of villages into first, second and third class was made according to the demand for land in each village.[29] Regard was also paid to the density of population in each village and the proportion between the settled and unsettled land in it.[30] Rules maintained the old division of land taken up for ordinary cultivation into (i) basti or garden land, (ii) rupit or transplanted rice land, and (iii) faringati or high land. But each of these classes was to be subdivided into first, second, and third classes, and if necessary into a fourth class and rates were to be different for different categories. Lands for special cultivation were settled under special rules.[31]

The settlement of 1893-94 raised the assessed revenue from 70 to 80 per cent in many cases. People throughout the Assam Valley protested vehemently against the measure, and sent memorials even to the Chief Commissioner Viceroy. But the administration put a deef ear to the grievances. The result was the outbreak of a series of agrarian riots in 1893-94. In Kamrup and Darrang, people soon organised campaign for non-payment of revenue and demonstrations.

The criterion of demand for land to assess revenue being found unsatisfactory, in the next settlement the principle was changed. The classification was to be in terms understood by the people and assessment rates were to be fixed strictly according to the relative value of the holders of the various classes of land. The rates of assessment were to be determined by the "soil unit" system.[32] In the district of Kamrup, resettlement took place between 1902-1905.[33] Lands were mainly divided into four classes, namely, basti, rupit, baotali, and faringati and then sub-divided into other categories. In Sibsagar, lands were divided into 13 classes after resettlement between 1902-1906.[34] The settlements of Darrang and Nowgong took place in 1908 and 1909 and that of Lakhimpur in 1911 and 1912. This setlement was made for 20 years. But all lands taken up from waste on periodic lease after the settlement was liable to revision in or after 11th year.

Sylhet and three thanas of Goalpara, Dhubri and Kailabor of Goalpara district were permanently settled.[35] But of the five duars of Goalpara Chirang, Ripu and Guma for revenue purposes treated like Assam proper. Bijni and Saldi were 'acknowledge estates' but subject to periodic settlement.[36]

There were some special revenue paying estates in Assam proper, namely, Chamua, Khat, Six-pie Lakhiraj and Tentwenties of Sibsagar.[37] A Chamua was a large holding under the Government paying full-revenue, but the Chamuadar had the privilege of paying the revenue direct to the treasury. Khats were grants of land enjoyed by Ahom dignitaries heriditarily but the revenue was assessed and realised by a special procedure. Some temple lands in Darrang paid revenue at the rate of Six-pie per bigha of cultivated lands. These were known as Lakhiraj tenure. In Sibsagar some princes enjoyed a special concession. Half the land revenue was remitted when revenue exceeded Rs. 20 but where the assessed revenue was more than Rs. 10 but less than Rs. 20 half the excess over Rs. 10 was remitted. The concession was for the lifetime of the land-holder but the two religious holdings enjoyed it perpetually.

Besides these were some Nisf-Khiraj or half revenue paying estates Debuttar, Brahmuttar and Dharmuttar were Nisf-Khiraj tenures.[38] They were again sub-divided into Bhogdhani and Paikan.

As a matter of policy, to encourage investors to take up land for cultivation of tea and coffee, Waste Land Grant Rules were passed from time to time since 1838.[39] Under these some land of a lease was held revenue free while others yielded revenue gradually after certain period. Rules were revised in 1854, 1861, 1874 and 1876.[40]

As in other classes of lands, there had been a gradual development of rules for the settlement of town lands as well. Formerly district and sub-divisional headquarters were regarded as towns but Assam Land and Revenue regulation included Municipality or notified areas in this category. Town lands were divided into three categories, agricultural, residential and trade sites. Assessment was made from 33 to 50 per cent of the annual value of land and resettlement took place after 30 years.[41] Lands available for settlement were either auctioned or settled at a premium.[42]

Finally, there were throughout the province a number of estates held directly from the Government under special conditions.[43]

The system of land revenue settlement in Assam except in the permanently settled tracts of Sylhet and Goalpara was Ryotwari. The most distinctive feature of Ryotwari system was the right to possess land covered by his pattah as long as he regularly paid the revenue. Right of inheritance was recognised tacitly and right of transfer was recognised provided it was registered properly. Government could resume land for public purposes paying compensation for houses or trees or crops on the land. In a word Government dealt with the ryot directly. But it did not mean that there was no sub-letting or intermediate tenancies. Rather with the increase of land value under the British administration sub-letting became exceedingly common. The assessment under this system was fixed on land and was paid by the cultivator proprietor for the time being. He was at liberty to relinquish his holding or part of it provided he served proper notice or could add to it by taking up waste land as opportunity arose. The settlement was revised periodically.

These periodic settlements were of great importance from administrative point of view. Before every settlement the Settlement Staff made a detailed inspection of every village and thus made it possible to acquire an intimate knowledge of the requirements and sentiments of the villagers.[44] Every re-settlement was preceded by an elaborate economic survey of the district, and the report of the survey was the most valuable document throwing light upon the economic condition of the country.[45] As land revenue constituted the bulk of the finance of the Government, preparation and preservation of Land Records after proper survey was a pre-requisite for the successful administration of land revenue. Before every fresh assessment a cadastral map and record had to be prepared and changes which occurred between one assessment and another had to be recorded. The object of this record was to show from whom the assessment of each holding or field was to be realised. The Government had decided to follow the principle of periodic settlement, arrangement had to be made to maintain records of all fiscal changes upto date accurately and the tenants were required to register all changes of title under penalties with the proper authorities.

Survey

Revenue survey of Assam proper was undertaken before it was formed into a Chief Commissionership and completed shortly after 1874.[46] In this survey the boundary of the villages, some tea grants, revenue free estates as well as geographical and topographical features were mapped on the scale of 1"—1 on plane table. But except in Jaintia parganas and Cachar no field survey was made.[47] The result of this survey, therefore, was of little practical value for revenue purposes.

In the permanently settled portion of the district of Sylhet survey was made by a non-professional party on the scale of 16"=1 mile. Though, inaccurate it was the only map of the district available.[48]

A cadastral survey based on regular professional traverse was undertaken for the first time in 1883, in the Assam Valley districts on the scale of 16"=1 mile and completed before 1893. Later this operation was extended to Sylhet and Cachar. Subsequently decision was taken to survey on theodolite traverse.[49] Since 1899 a permanent professional survey detachment was maintained in the province under the Director of Agriculture and Land Records.[50] In 1909-10, the survey detachment was merged into a separate survey department under a Surveyor General for Eastern Bengal and Assam. But after the restoration of the Chief Commissionership in 1912 the Superintendent of Survey Eastern Circle, Government of India, performed the duties of the Surveyor General with a party called Assam Traverse Party.[51]

Land records

In August, 1879, the Government of India undertook a review of agricultural conditions of country and arrived at a conclusion that failure to maintain correct agricultural records resulted in either serious financial loss to the Government or in the institution of operations which were harassing to the agricultural population. In 1881, the Secretary of the State for India sanctioned the reconstitution of the Department of Agriculture of the Government of India. The Government of India thereupon directed the provincial Governments and Administrations to set-up separate machinery for Agricultural affairs. The object was to aid first survey, classification of soil and fresh recording as fresh settlement was both expensive and unpopular. But the Government had definitely accepted the principle that assessment was liable to change but change would be necessary only to meet (i) an extension of cultivation, (ii) or an increase of produce due to improvement made by the State, (iii) or a rise in prices. Therefore, it was necessary to collect agricultural statistics and an accurate revenue register for each unit of revenue administration. The Secretary of State for India in despatch No. 67 of 26.9.1882 "fully shared the conviction of the Government of India as to the greatest advantages not confined to the facilitating and cheapening of settlement operations which will attend the continuous maintenance of agricultural records."[52]

On the recommendation of the Commission a Director of Agriculture and Land Records had already been appointed in Assam and the revenue establishment of the districts were then reorganised on a departmental basis under him. His main duty was to supervise Survey and Settlement operations but he was also entrusted with the collection of trade and agricultural statistics, the management of survey schools and similar works.[53] Under the system in force in Assam the land revenue assessment was, in a great measure, annually revised by the land records staff of the Sub-Deputy Collector, Kanungoos and Mandals. They surveyed the lands annually, issued leases of the lands newly taken up, tested the applications filed for the relinquishment of lands corrected the revenue rolls and recorded the areas under different crops.[54] Each district was divided into fiscal units of 5000 acres called circle under a local accountant called Mandal. Over every 20 or 25 Mandals there was a Kanungoo and over the Kanungoo of the district was the Sub-Deputy Collector. In the plains districts of the Brahmaputra Valley except Goalpara there was a Sub-Deputy Collector who was mainly employed upon the supervision over the revenue establishment and compilation of revenue records and returns after proper survey.[55]

But a system of continuous enquiry into agricultural conditions and recording of agricultural statistics was initiated in the Assam Valley only in 1897-98.[56] This was designed to provide a permanent source of information for general administrative and fiscal purposes and specially to afford a basis for the reassessment of land revenue demand at resettlement of Assam Valley districts.[57] This record which was known as Mouza book was introduced in all districts which came under resettlement.

Registration

The settlement Rule of 1870 declared lands settled for a term were transferable and heritable on condition on transfer being registered.[58] These principles were embodied into the land Revenue Regulation of 1886. So a system of registration had to be arranged all through the province. In the Brahmaputra Valley where there was less registration work, all subordinate magistrates were made ex-officio Sub-registrars.[59] They did registration work in addition to their other duties. But in the Surma Valley a separate staff for registration work was maintained. At every sub-divisional headquarters there was a Sub-Registrar's office and in some rural areas also Sub-Registrars were maintained.[60] But the Registration Act was inoperative in the hill districts.

ADMINISTRATION OF REVENUE

The distinguishing feature of the agricultural system was the large areas of unsettled waste land, and the system under which certain tracts of land was cultivated for two or three years and then resigned. As a matter of fact, the ryot was not subjected to any harassing restriction if he was willing to pay the revenue.

He held an annual or periodic lease from Government and was free to relinquish the whole or any part of his holding provided he served a proper notice. Any unoccupied waste land could be taken up for cultivation without notice or application and when so taken up, was settled with the occupant. Large areas of land was annually taken up and relinquished after one or two years where fluctuating cultivation was practised.

The system of land tenure and cultivation required a simple system of Land Revenue Administration for the province. In 1874, when Assam was constituted a Chief Commissionership it was not provided with a Board of Revenue. The Chief Commissioner was Local Government and Board of Revenue in Assam. In 1800, the Judge of the Assam Valley was appointed Commissioner. Since then the Chief Commissioner was relieved of works in the Assam Valley but he acted as Commissioner in the Hill districts and in the Surma Valley.[61] During the period when Assam formed a part of the province of Eastern Bengal and Assam (1905-1912), a general control over the greater part of revenue was entrusted to a Board of Revenue which consisted of two members who exercised full powers independently of one another each being the head of the department committed to his charge.[62] Next to the Chief Commissioner there were the Deputy Commissioners, Assistant Commissioners and Extra Assistant Commissioners of the Districts.[63] They were the ex-officio revenue officers of the district. An Assistant Commissioner or the Extra Assistant Commissioner when in charge of a sub-division was styled Sub-Divisional Officer. Below them there were Sub-Deputy Collector, Tehsildar (including Naib Tehsildars), Mouzadars, in Assam Valley, Revenue Nazirs including Naib Nazir and such other officers as were authorised to receive payment of land revenue or other currency realisable under revenue regulations.[64]

We have already noted that the province was divided into districts and districts into Sub-Divisions which in their turn for fiscal purposes into circles and mouzas. In 1880 the six plains districts of Assam Valley were constituted into a Commissionership which was united with the Judgeship of the Assam Valley districts. Thus at the top of the Revenue administration of the province stood the Chief Commissioner,[65] who was the supreme authority subject nominally to the Governor-General-in-Council

Next came the Commissioner between the Chief Commissioner and the Deputy Commissioner in the Assam Valley. In the districts the Deputy Commissioner was the Collector and he was assisted by Assistant and Extra Assisstant Commissioners who were his Assistant Collectors.[66] Then there were Sub-Deputy Collectors, in each sub-division who supervised the collection of local officers like the Mouzadar in the Assam Valley and the Tehsildar in the Surma Valley district. Each of these officers had definite duties and powers with regard to revenue administration.

The Divisional Commissioner was required to perform the duties defined in the Rules of the Board of Revenue, Lower Provinces, so far as these rules were applicable, and modified by any special orders of the Chief Commissioner.[67] He controlled, supervised and inspected the Collector's revenue works. He was given the power to sanction the remission of revenue on temporarily settled lands.[68] He appointed petty revenue affairs like the Mouzadar and Mandals. He heared appeals against the decision of the District Officers in matters of land revenue. All revenue reports and returns of the districts were also sent through him.[69] The Deputy Commissioner was the head of the revenue department of the district, and through his subordinates he was in touch with every inch of territory of the district. As collector he was responsible for the collection of land revenue both of agricultural and non-agricultural land in the district and also forest revenue.[70] It was his duty to administer Watan Act, that is Inams and to make grants to agriculturists in times of need from the Government fund. As collector he was in charge of the treasury and was responsible for the due accounting of all money received and disbursed, the correct ness of revenue returns and the safe custody of valuables which it contained. As the collector, the Deputy Commissioner was to try rent suits and was also the Registrar of the district. During a large part of the year he had to tour different villages in his district to supervise the work of his subordinates and get into direct touch with the people and the problems of administration.[71]

Assistant and Extra Assistant Commissioners under training were employed during the cold weather entirely upon revenue and settlement duties in the interior.[72] Assistant Commissioners were employed in examining and attesting the periodical returns despatched from revenue office which gave a good practical knowledge of revenue works. They were further employed in examining the record rooms and seeing that the record were properly maintained. The Assistant Commissioner was required to acquire a sound knowledge of settlement and survey details and as such he was attached to survey and settlement parties as and when opportunities occurred. The Deputy Commissioner of the district during the cold weather assigned to Assistant Commissioners of his district such duties as would qualify them to become good Settlement Officers. They decided questions of boundary disputes making use of thakbast, cadastral and other survey maps. An Assistant was expected to take his first lesson from an Extra Assistant and Sub-Deputy Collector who were actually employed in settlement duties and he was required to draw up a report of the settlement as finally made to prove that he had entered into and understood the different processes. At the end of every year a special report was prepared and submitted showing the employment and proficiency of the Assistant Commissioner. Special aptitudes of such officers were to be recorded in the annual Land Revenue Report.[73]

At the lowest rung of the revenue administration were the Mouzadars and Mandals in the Assam Valley and Tehsildars and Patwaris in the Surma Valley. They were both revenue and settlement officers. The average area under a Mouzadar varied from 44 square miles in the district of Sibsagar to 64 square miles in the district of Darrang.[74] And the average area assigned to a Mandal varied from 13 square miles in the district of Sibsagar to 41 square miles in the district of Lakhimpur. In the Eastern Duars the average jurisdiction of a Mouzadar and Mandal were 98 and 62 square miles respectively.[75] The duties of these officers were of extremely varied nature. A Mouzadar was not only the Settlement Officer who was to test the field operation of the Mandals and supervise Kanungoo and Collecting agency, but he was a man of various works. He had to report on criminal complaints and on questions arising out of "patta-cases." He was required to supply labour, bamboos, nusud etc, the census work was also entrusted to him. In matters of general administration when the District Officer and his subordinates did not know what to do in a particular case, they sought consolation and solution of their problems in a "Kaifyat" from the Mouzadar.[76] They mainly depended upon the reports of the Mandal for the collection of revenue and had less time to supervise their work.[77]

Though the Mouzadar is the main prop of the Revenue system of the province, he was not on the pay of the government. The Mouzadar was remunerated by a commission of 10 per cent on the collection of Rs. 10,000 and 6 per cent on the subsequent amount.[78] Usually local people of standing in society were appointed as Mouzadar. In appointing the son of the previous Mouzadar was preferred. Often the Mouzadar was illiterate. The Government rule provided that if he was illiterate he was to engage an Amin to help in settlement operation. In practice this rule was not insisted upon. The Mouzadar was assisted by his Muharrir. Sometimes the Mouzadar did not reside in his Mouza. Sometimes Mouzadars were outsiders. So in 1883 ultimately the Government decided to replace the Mouzadary system by establishing Tehsil system that existed in Upper India. Several Mouzas were amalgamated and made into a circle over which a Tehsildar on a fixed salary was appointed The Tehsildar was a Government Officer with good academic qualifications.[79]

But the Mouzadary system was much popular and well-understood by the people. Allthough it was rough and ready, it was cheap and not oppressive. The Commissioner of Assam Valley division Maxwell wrote in the Administration Report for the year 1896-97. "One native gentleman whose ideas are much in advance of his countrymen was of opinion that the Mouzadary system was better suited to the people, the Mouzadar was an inhabitant of the area, ... he was respected by the ryots and assisted them in times of distress, and generally speaking was their adviser in family disputes".[80] Still the same Officer was of opinion that "comparing the cost of collection by Tehsildars with that of Mouzadars, the tehsildary system is decidedly an improvement over the mouzadary system. The Tehsildars are a better class of officers than the latter". Duties remaining almost the same the Tehsildars performed them in a much better way and they were real help to district officers in the administration ef revenue.[81]

But the Tehsildary system led to great areas and remissions.[82] It proved less popular owing to the distance which the people had to travel to pay the revenue. The Deputy Commissioner of Goalpara reported in his administration report "Mr. Campbell who has great experience of this district and its requirement and system of administration considered that the present Mouzadars were well suited for work required of them. Mr. Murray, his successor characterised the Mouzadars as ignorent men with little or no knowledge of mensuration and with but little capacity for account, but he generally agreed with Campbell. With my short experience I do not think I should condemn them as a body."[83] As late as 1897-98 P.G. Militus, Commissioner of Assam Valley district wrote that tehsil system was not much cheaper as it at first sight appeared to be.[84] Moreover whatever savings were effected did not compensate the loss of political and administrative advantage of Mouzadary system. Therefore from 1893 again Mouzadary system was reintroduced.[85]

The Mandal stood at the lowest rank of the revenue Administration and yet he was the pivot of the entire system. His responsibilities were too heavy and yet he was the lowest paid officer. The Mandal was the village accountant who visited the fields, surveyed all lands, prepared Dagchetha and Jamabandi and distributed Pattahs to the ryots. He was required to undertake field survey before he prepared his dagchitha and Jamabandi and take into account all relinquishments of lands, new land taken up for cultivation and the various areas under different crops. Moreover, he was put under the survilence of the Kanungoo, Mouzadar and Tehsildars. The Mouzadar and Tehsildar relied upon him for the collection of rent.[86]

But the pay of the Mandal was extremely poor and little wonder that he supplemented it by illegal exaction from the tenants. Mr. Ward recommended to replace the Mandals by a commission as the Mouzadars were paid but the Chief Commissioner negatived the proposal. Instead the Mandals were graded into three classes. Honest and efficient Mandals were thus offered a prospect of promotion.[87]

Over the Mandals there was a Supervisor Kanungoo. This Officer was held strictly responsible to see that all changes were correctly recorded by the Mandals. He was also required to test the field survey made by the Mandal and examine the pattahs. He was required to go on tour to make enquiries during the days of Jamabandi.[88]

Though the Mouzadar and Tehsildar were to scrutinise and supervise the work of the Mandals in their respective jurisdiction, a special settlement officer was appointed in each district to carry out the settlement and revenue administration. Mr. Ward had recommended in his annual report in 1881-82 that arrangement should be made to appoint for each district Settlement Officer who will give to Mouzadars and Mandals to understand that their papers were subject to closest scrutiny and that enquiry would be made not only to test the measurement but also to ascertain whether all lands had been measured properly. The rules issued in 1892 authorised the Sub-Deputy Collectors in charge of revenue administration of the district to see that Mandals, Kanungoos, Mouzadars and Tehsildars act properly as per requirements and submitted returns punctually. He was also required to undertake tours to supervise the working of the subordinate agency, scrutinise their papers, and submit statements of his visits.[89]

Finally, the village institution of Gaonbura was utilised for revenue administration as well. As the Gaonbura was a respectable man, the Government invested the Gaonbura formally as a Government Officer and remunerated him by a remission of land revenue.[90] The revenue officers called upon him for necessary help in times of tour in the particular village.

Collection of revenue

The original system of collection of land revenue in the Brahmaputra Valley and Cachar was one under which an individual of wealth and local standing entered into a contract with the Government to pay the land revenue of one or more mouzas or fiscal units. He did not have any interest in land but enjoyed the profits that accrued from the extension of cultivation.[92] But later on settlement with such contractors was made annually and he was remunerated by a commission of 10 per cent on collection. Survey or assessment works were done by a separate staff.[93] Since 1882 there was an attempt to introduce the tehsil system under which revenue officers for each circle styled Tehsildar were appointed on fixed salary. But in 1893 the old mouzadari system was revived as we have already noted.

The cultivator was required to pay the revenue on fixed days.[94]. If he failed to pay it a demand notice was served upon him. This rule had the desired effect, but in case of recusancy, the movable property of the defaulter and even the land of the cultivator could be attached.[95]

In the Garo, Jaintia, Naga Hills, North Cachar and in few villages in the Khasi Hills, the house tax was collected by the village headmen known as Laskars and Lukmas in the Garo Hills, Dulloi and Sardars in the Jaintia and Khasi Hills, Lambardar in Naga Hills and Mouzadars in Cachar Hills. These officers were also remunerated by a commission like the Mouzadars of the Assam Valley.[96]

In the permanently settled areas of Goalpara people paid revenue directly to the treasury situated at the headquarters of the district. In Sylhet, there was a collecting office at the head-quarter of every sub-division where revenue was paid. In the plain portions of Cachar there were also three tehsils or collecting establishment which received the revenue.[97] The only portion of the assessed areas of the Assam Valley which were exempt from paying the revenue through the Mouzadars were certain communities of Miris in Lakhimpur who paid poll-tax through their headmen, the Waste Land Grants, held chiefly by the Tea Planters, and the large estates held by privileged tenants on payment of ordinary rates of land revenue. They paid direct into the treasury.[98]

The land revenue was mainly a heritage from the indigenous rule but the administration of land revenue was a natural growth of the substitution of monetary payment in the place of manual labour. Starting with a fairly detailed knowledge of the practice during the Ahom rule, the Anglo-Indian administrators built the present complex of the land revenue administration in Assam.

But the revenue policy of the Government does not seem to be popular one. The periodical enhancement of revenue based upon statistical data without ascertaining real improvement in the economic condition of the people was a constant source of worry and apprehension to the people.[99] Popular discontent increased not only for enhancement of revenue at every resettlement but for imposition of new taxes such as Stamp Duty, Licence fee for collecting forest products etc.[100] But then the relieving features use the concession to abandon land taken up for cultivation with due notice, the progressive rate of revenue assessment for fallow lands and the procedure for collection through the Mouzadars.

REFERENCES

1. Barpuzari, H.K.: *Assam in the Days of the Company*, p. 26.
2. Saikia, K.N.: *The Assam Land and Revenue Regulation*, 1886, p. 10.
3. Ibid., 1886, p. 10.
4. The Assam Land Revenue Manual, Vol. I, p. liv.
5. Barpuzari, H.K.: *Assam in the Days of the Company*, p. 25.
6. Ibid.
7. Ibid.
8. The Assam Land Revenue Manual, Vol. I, p. liv.
9. Ibid., p. lv.
10. Ibid., p. lv.
11. Saikia, K.N.: *The Assam Land and Revenue Regulation*, 1886, p. 11.
12. The Assam Land Revenue Manual, Vol. I, p. iv.
13. Saikia, K.N.: *The Assam Land and Revenue Regulation*, 1886, p. 11.
14. The Assam Land Revenue Manual, Vol. I, p. lvi.
15. Ibid, p. lviii.
16. Saikia, K.N.: *The Assam Land and Revenue Regulation*, 1886, p. 14
17. Ibid, p. 14.
18. Ibid., 1886, p. 15.
19. The Assam Land Revenue Manual, Vol. 1, p. lix.
20. Ibid., p. ix.
21. Ibid, p. lix.
22. Ibid, p. llx.
23. Ibid, p. ix.
24. Ibid., Vol. I, p. lix.
25. Ibid., p. lx.
26. Assam Valley Reassessment Report 1892-93.
27. Ibid.
28. The Assam Land Revenue Manual, Vol. I, p. lxvii.
29. Ibid, p. lxvi.
30. Assam Valley Reassessment Report, 1892-93.
31. Ibid.
32. Saikia, K.N.: The Assam Land and Revenue Regulation, 1886, p. 17.
33. Ibid., 1886, p. 17.
34. Ibid, p. 17.
35. RAA 1921-22, part II, para 138.
36. Saikia, K.N.: *The Assam Land and Revenue Regulation*, 1886, p: 17.
37. Ibid, p. 17.

38. The Assam Land Revenue Manual, Vol. I, p. xli, p. xcixv.
39. Ibid., p. xivi.
40. Ibid., p. xcii.
41. Saikia, K.N.: *The Assam Land and Revenue Regulation*, 1886, p. 17.
42. Ibid., p. 23.
43. Ibid., p. 24.
44. Ibid., 1886, p. 48.
45. Ibid., p. 26.
46. Imperial Gazatteer, Vol. VI, p. 107.
47. Ibid., p. 108.
48. Ibid.
49. Ibid.
50. RAA 1921-22, part II, para, 139.
51. Ibid., para 135.
52. RAA 1921-22. part II, para, 139.
53. RAA 1901-02, part II, para 109.
54. Ibid., part II, para 201.
55. Imperial Gazatteer, Vol. IV, p. 89.
56. RAA, 1901-02, part II, para 201.
57. Ibid., para 201.
58. RAA 1874-75, part IIA, para 214.
59. RAA 1901-02, part II, para 112.
60. Ibid., para 112.
61. RAA 1874-76, part IIB, para 2.
62. RAA 1882-83, part II, para 104.
63. RAEBA, 1905-06, part II, para 125.
64. RAA 1882-83, part II, para, 104.
65. The Assam Land and Revenue Regulation, 1886, Rule 122.
66. Ibid., Rule 123.
67. RAR 1880-81, para 25.
68. PGAJD No. 94 of June, 1880.
69. Ibid.
70. RAR 1880-81, para 97.
71. RAR 1882-83, para 105.
72. RAR 1880-81, para 25.
73. Manual of Executive Rules and Orders in force in Assam, p. 89.
74. RAR 1882-83, para 104.
75. RAR 1880-81, para 97.
76. Ibid., para 97.
77. RAR 1882-83, para, 108.
78. Ibid.
79. RAA 1880-81, part II, para 2.
80. Ibid., para 2.
81. RAR 1882-83, para 108.
82. Ibid.
83. RAA 1880-81, part II, para 2.
84. Ibid., para 2.

85. Ibid., para 2.
86. Imperial Gazatteer, Vol. IV, p. 50.
87. Ibid., p. 50.
88. Manual of Executive Rules and Orders, p. 89.
89. Ibid., p. 89.
90. RAR 1880-81, para 25.
91. RAR 1896-97, para 53.
92. Ibid., para 53.
93. Ibid., para 53.
94. Ibid.
95. RAR 1880-81, para 25.
96. RAR 1896-97, para 63.
97. Ibid., para 53.
98. RAR of 1896-97, para 53.
99. Dutt, K.N.: *Land Marks of the Freedom Movement in Assam*, p. 28.
100. Ibid., p. 25.

6

ADMINISTRATION OF JUSTICE

THE BRITISH came to India at a time when the Mughal Empire was distintegrating and chaos and confusion had set in. As conquerors of the country they were called upon to restore law and order to protect life, liberty and property of the people. To enforce law and order, police stations and courts were established. The judicature which they established was especially charged with the duty of preserving the liberties, the privileges and the rights which they conferred upon their subjects.

The same was the case in Assam. The British came to Assam when the Ahom administration was collapsing and justice disappearing. They were called upon to guarantee individual liberty, privileges and rights. In this they showed sagacity. They studied the existing conditions before introducing any change in the existing system of administration so that no trouble might arise. Though they had obtained the Dewani of Bengal Subah in 1765, it was in 1773 that they took over revenue management and civil administration and in 1790 the Nizamat or criminal administration.[1] In Assam immediately after its annexation they did not introduce any radical change in the administrative system. An Agent to Governor-General and Commissioner was putin charge of the newly acquired non-regulated territories.

Gradually, however, the Commissioner appointed Assistants for the administration of justice and for the collection of revenue. But for the purpose of dispensing justice the British initially made use of the "Khel" and the "Mel" system.[2] The officers of the "Khel" were empowered to try cases of petty nature with the aid of "Mels" while the serious offences and claims of larger amounts were tried by the Assistants of the Commissioners.[3]

Administration of justice, Ahom period

During the Ahom period there was no separate judicial service. Further no distinction was made between civil and criminal cases. Small disputes were tried by persons under whom "Pykes" of the crown were placed. The power of inflicting punishment was reserved for the principal officers of the crown and the Raja. In regard to civil cases an appeal could be taken to the three provincial courts where the Bara Barua, Bora Phukan and Sadiya Khowa Gohain presided.[4] They had full jurisdiction in all cases civil and criminal and could inflict punishment short of death without reference to the King, but no person could be put to death without an order from the King and that order was procured by sending an account of the proceedings in writing.[5] A second appeal could be made to the King which was dealt with on his behalf and in his absence by the Nyaya Sodha Phukan created in the reign of Rudra Singh.[6]

In the administration of justice witnesses were examined and written documents were received in evidence. Judges decided cases according to the customs of the country. No written laws existed previous to the introduction of Brahmanical religion. The monarch could take congnizance of any case in his kingdom. No record was maintained in regard to criminal trials. In regard to civil cases a summary of the proceedings was drawn up and delivered to the successful party. The president of the court was assisted by a number of assessors called Katakis, Ganaks and Pundits by whose opinion he was usually guided.[7]

Administration of justice upto 1874

The system devised by Mr. David Scott empowered the Choudhuries, Rajas and other revenue officers to try petty cases, both civil and criminal in Lower Assam. More serious cases were tried by the Commissioner himself and by his only Assistant. With the increase in the number of cases, elected mufassil panchayats were created and three native courts were provisionally established.[8] The first court of these sort consisted of a Rajkhowa and three assessors. It had jurisdiction over civil cases involving not more than rupees one hundred and fifty, the second court consisted of one Barphukan and three assessors. It had original jurisdiction in cases involving more than rupees one hundred fifty but not more than one thousand and appeallate jurisdiction over cases from lower courts; the third similarly constituted tried criminal cases of minor importance and heard appeals from Rajas, Choudhuries and other revenue officials who were empowered to try cases. A Bar Panchayat or court for trial of heinous offences not cognizable by the Commissioner was set-up consisting of three native judges aided by two pundits and six assessors. These officers were to apprehend crime and convict offenders and to exercise authority and perform functions of a Zila Magistrate. They were empowered to inflict a sentence involving imprisonment for not more than three years, subject to an appeal to the Commissioner. In regard to grave and more serious cases proceedings along with the opinion and findings of the court were to be transmitted to the Commissioner, who had power to review punishment proposed and inflict a sentence of death without previous reference to the Supreme Government.[9]

In Upper Assam, for the trial of civil cases, Landlord Barphukan, a brother-in-law of ex-Raja Chandra Kanta was appointed co-adjutor with the Barbarua of the revenue department. Some Surasuree Panchayats consisting of former pundits were also instituted to decide suits of minor importance.[10] Criminal cases were tried by the Junior Commissioner and after restoration of Chandra Kanta by the Political Agent or by the Barphukan who was empowered to pass a sentence of 30 stripes, an imprisonment for six months or a fine not exceeding rupees fifty Heinous offences were tried with the help of juries Barphukan presiding, but the sentence was subject to the appeal for the Commissioner.[11]

Act II of 1835 placed Assam under Sadar Court in regard to the administration of civil and criminal justice and under Board of Revenue of Bengal in regard to fiscal matters.[12] The Sadar Court promulgated a Code known as Assam Code in 1837.[13] The Assam Code determined the courts, civil and criminal that should be established and the mode of appointing judicial officers. It also determined the jurisdiction of these courts and provided for an appeal. These rules were revised in 1847. They were in force till they were superseded by the Civil Procedure Code (Act VII of 1859) on 26 April 1860 ond Criminal Procedure Code (Act XXV of 1861) on 1 January, 1862.[14]

Meanwhile, Lower Assam was divided into four districts and after Chandra Kanta was expelled. Upper Assam also was divided into two districts. In each district an officer called Principal Assistant to the Commissioner was appointed. Judicial, magisterial and revenue functions were vested in him. The Principal Assistant was assisted by Junior Assistant who was subordinate to him. Some districts were divided into sub-divisions. Each sub-division was in charge of a Junior Assistant.

The Principal Assistants had jurisdiction over both civil and criminal cases. In regard to civil suits, he had original jurisdiction over all cases whose value was not less than rupees two hundred but not more than one thousand and appellate jurisdiction over all appeals from the Lower Courts. All suits exceeding rupees one thousand and special appeals had to be referred to the Commissioner. In each district there existed two other courts. The Munsif's court vested with the power of trying all original suits involving rupees one hundred to five hundred whether of personal or of real property and to hear appeals from Panchayats vested with the powers of trying suits upto rupees one hundred. In criminal cases, the Principal Assistants exercised the authority of a Magistrate of Bengal with the additional duties of investigating heinous crimes with the aid of a jury.[15] After investigation, the proceedings had to be transmitted to the court of the Commissioners to which the verdict of the jury and the remarks of the Magistrate thereon, were sent for final orders.

The Assam Code of 1837 empowered the Principal Assistant to try any civil case. He was authorised to transfer cases to the subordinate courts to withdraw any case from any tribunal and try them personally or refer them to some other courts. An appeal against the decision of the Principal Assistant lay with the Commissioner. Special appeals could be taken to the Sadar Court. In the regulated districts appeal against the decision of a case the value of which exceeded rupees ten thousand could be taken to the Privy Council : but such cases under modified rules were tried by the Assistant himself or forwarded to Sadar Dewani Adalat. In 1839 to relieve congestion at the Sadar Court the Junior or sub-Assistants were vested with more enlarged powers. They were vested with the powers of a collector to try all cases under their jurisdiction, whether of summary suit of arrears, exactions, over assessment or miscellaneous character, and appeals against their decision, could be taken to the Commissioner.[16]

In criminal cases, persons charged with murder and other heinous crimes continued to be tried by Principal Assistant with or without the aid of a jury. In the event of disagreement, between the court and the jury the presiding officer forwarded the proceedings with his remarks to the Deputy Commissioner who was vested with the power of a District and Sessions Judge. All sentences of imprisonment for life, sentences of death and punishment for offences against the State to be confined by Sadar Court which was the highest court of justice. The Junior Assistant exercised the same powers in criminal cases as the Deputy Magistrate of Bengal, but the uncovenanted Sub-Assistant and the Sadar Amin had only limited jurisdiction and other cases involving petty thefts and other minor offences referred to them by the Principal Assistant and cases in which punishment of more than a month's imprisonment with or without labour, or a fine of more than rupees fifty confirmation by the Sadar Court was not necessary.[17]

In the Hill areas petty cases were tried by the village headmen while more serious cases were tried by the Principal Assistant and Junior Assistant. So Sadar Court had no jurisdiction over the hill districts.[18] The Commissioner was the highest court of appeal so for as hill areas were concerned.[19]

For the trial of the British born subjects no provision existed in the districts. In cases of breach of law on their part, they were to be sent under proper custody to Calcutta to be tried there by the Supreme Court of judicature.

After the Sepoy mutiny a series of changes were made in the organization of courts. In 1860, Act VIII of 1859 was extended to the whole of the Brahmaputra Valley.[20] In 1861, the designation and duties of judicial officers were changed. The Senior or Principal Assistant become Deputy Commissioner, the Junior

Assistant become Assistant Commissioner.[26] In 1872, judicial establishment of principal Sadar Amins, Sadar Amins and Munsif were abolished by the Bengal Government.[22] The Deputy Commissioner was vested with the powers of a Subordinate Judge and the Assistant and Extra Assistant Commissioner were given the powers of a Munsif under Section 10 of Act VI of 1871.[23] The Government of India approved these changes in May 1875.[24]

Development after 1874

When Assam was constituted into a Chief Commissionership 1874, the jurisdiction of the High Court of Calcutta was retained.[25] The judicial staff of the province in 1874-75 consisted of two Judges, eleven Deputy Commissioners, eighteen Assistant Commissioners, twenty-four Extra Assistant Commissioners, Eight Subordinate Judges in Sylhet, two Sub-Deputy Collectors in Sylhet, and a special establishment of one Assistant Commissioner.[26] The number of Honorary Magistrates was twenty-five.[27] Judicial powers, both civil and criminal, were exercised by Deputy Commissioners, Assistant Commissioners in addition to their administrative duties.[28] In Sylhet alone, the lower grades of judicial officers performed no administrative functions.[29] The power and authority of Civil and Sessions Judge for all the districts of Assam Valley were proposed to be centred in one officer known as the Judicial Commissioner.[30] The Judge of Sylhet was also the Sessions Judge of Cachar but had no jurisdiction in that district over civil cases, the functions of the Civil Judge there devolving on the Deputy Commissioner. Judges of Assam were borne on the Bengal list.[31]

The judiciary of the Assam Valley districts was reorganised in May 1875, by a notification of the Government of India. The Judicial Commissioner of the Assam Valley districts was now designated as the Judge of the Assam Valley districts. He was vested with the power of a District Judge. The Deputy Commissioners of those districts and officers in charge of the sub-divisions of Dhubri, Mangaldoi, Jorhat and North Lakhimpur were vested with the powers of a Subordinate Judge and the Senior Assistant Commissioners at each of the six headquarters stations and the Officer in charge of all the sub-divisions were vested with the powers of a Munsif.[32]

Civil justice

For the administration of civil justice there were three types of courts. At the apex was the District Judges court headed by the District and Sessions Judge, next came the courts of the Subordinate Judges of the districts. Below the district and Subordinate Courts there were courts of Munsifs. The Subordinate and District Judges and Jurisdiction over all original suits cognizable by the Civil Courts. The jurisdiction of a Munsif Court extended to all cases the value of which did not exceed one thousand rupees. However, the value of the suits in dispute in the court of Munsif could be raised to two thousand rupees by the Local Government.[33] An appeal against the decision could be taken to the Subordinate Judge. Appeal against the decision of the Subordinate Judge except in cases in which the value exceeded rupees five thousand. In the latter case appeal was taken to the High Court in Calcutta. An appeal from the decision of the High Court was taken to the Privy Council if the value of the case exceeded rupees ten thousand.[34]

Besides there existed "small cause courts" for the summary disposal of petty cases. These cases were generally disposed of by the Subordinate Judge and Munsif. Subject to certain exceptions the jurisdiction of small cause courts extended to all suits of civil nature the value of which did not exceed rupees five hundred, a limit which could be raised upto one thousand by the Local Government.[35]

The number of civil cases increased steadily both in the Assam and in the Surma Valley districts. But the strength of the judiciary did not increase proportionately. In 1874, the total number of cases instituted was 19,791 of which 6,604 were contested. In 1875, the figure was 21,311 of which 7,650 were contested.[36] The average time taken for decision of civil cases in 1874 was two months whereas in 1875 it came to 63 days.[37]

The number of civil suits instituted in 1881 was 22,549,[38] in 1892, 22975,[39] in 1901, 28,870,[40] in 1912, 34,679, in 1920, 47,741.[42] In 1881 Munsifs in Assam Valley disposed of 727 cases each on the average. In the Surma Valley each Munsif disposed of 1,303 cases as they were engaged only for judicial work.[43] Moreover, the Sub-Judge of Sylhet disposed of 494 cases and the Sub-Judge of Assam Valley disposed 252 cases each.[44]

In 1892 for decision of a case before Munsif it took 80 days for cases contested and 44 for uncontested[45] and in 1901 it came to 110 days and 52 days respectively.[46]

The income of the Government from the administration of justice usually showed a surplus of income over expenditure. The surplus of income over expenditure for the administration of justice was Rs. 1,02,068 in 1881,[47] Rs. 45,453 in 1891, in the Assam Valley, Rs. 63,302 in Sylhet and Rs 4,951[48] in Cachar, in 1901 the total surplus came to Rs. 1,77,755[49] in 1912 Rs. 3,01,219,[50] and even in 1920 Rs. 5,12,467 surplus.[51]

The staff position did not change substantially. In 1920 we find two Judges, one Additional District Judge, ten Sub-Judges and twenty-seven Munsifs in the province. In 1920, one Additional Sub-Judge was appointed in the Assam Valley.[52] The staff was therefore inadequate and as a consequence the administration of justice was very slow and costly.

Criminal justice

For the administration of criminal justice there were two types of courts. The first administered general criminal laws, the second administered special rules sanctioned by the High Court of Calcutta.[53] In the first class were included the courts of the eight plain districts and in the second the court of the three hills district courts, in which the Chief Commissioner was the Highest Court of Appeal. The High Court of Calcutta had no jurisdiction over them.[54] The eight plain districts were divided into three session divisions. The six Brahmaputra Valley districts comprised one session division over which was appointed a District and Sessions Judge. Sylhet formed another sessions division and Cachar the third.[55] For Sylhet and Cachar one District and Sessions Judge was appointed.

Stipendary Magistrates were the foundation of the administration of criminal justice though a few Honorary Magistrates were appointed from time to time.[54] The stipendary Magistrates were divided into three classes. They were vested with first, second and third class powers.[56] The highest punishment that a First Class Magistrate could inflict was imprisonment for two years either simple or rigorous and a fine upto Rs. 1,000, the Second Class Magistrate could award a punishment of imprisonment upto six months, either simple or rigorous and a fine upto

Rs. 200, and a Third Class Magistrate could award a sentence of one month imprisonment, simple or rigorous, and/or a fine upto Rs. 100.[57] Offences deserving more severe punishment or too heinous were tried by the District and Sessions Judges. But death sentences passed by them required confirmation by the High Court of Calcutta.[58] In the Assam Valley districts, offences under Chapters VIII, XI, XVI, XVII, XVIII of Indian Penal Code were tried with the aid of Jurors and other sessions cases with the aid of Assessors.[59] In Sylhet the Sessions cases were tried with the help of Assessors.[60]

Appeals from the decision of the Magistrates could be taken to the Sessions Judge except in the case of Magistrates of the second and third class powers from whom an appeal was taken to the District Magistrate or a Magistrate who was specially invested for that purpose. Appeals from the Sessions Judge were taken to the High Court of Calcutta.[61]

Comparatively crime in Assam was less, particularly in the Assam Valley. In 1880, the total number of cases instituted were 24,049,[62] in 1891 it increased to 64,412,[63] in 1901, 30,476[64], in 1912, 35,983[65] and in 1920, 46,048.[66] The rise of crime incidence was due to many factors like increase in population, consciousness of the people to report crime to Police Stations, increase in the number of Police Staff and easy accessibity of stations. But the number of Judges remained almost stationary and as a consequence there was delay in the disposal of cases. Sessions cases, particularly in the Assam Valley, took a long time for decision. In 1881, the average duration of a sessions case was 69.9 days in Assam Valley, it was longest in the Sibsagar district where it was 111 days.[67]

But revenue from the administration of criminal justice increased steadily. In 1880, it was Rs. 1,03,690,[68] in 1892 it was Rs. 10,752[69] and in 1901 Rs. 2,40,006.[70]

Of witnesses that were summoned to give evidence 18 per cent were detained for more than one day in 1881.[71] In 1892-93 of the 64,412 witness summoned, 83.3 per cent were examined on the first day, and 2.05 per cent on the third day.[72] The witness, of course, was paid travel expenses by appropriate class as well as compensation for his other professional loss.[73]

But an attempt of the Government to create one more Judgeship in the Assam Valley met with opposition from the people. Meetings were held to protest against the measure.[74] The opposition was not because people wanted delayed justice but they did not wish litigation and further increase of the European officers.[75] Any addition to Session Judgeship meant an increase of European officers which people at that time hardly desired.

The system of trials by the Jury in the Assam Valley districts was in general successful. In 1874, out of 20 cases tried with the help of Jury the judge, agreed with the verdict of the Jury in 19 cases. In 1875, he agreed with the Jury in all the 11 cases that came up for trial before the jury.[76] In 1911-12, out of 85 cases, the Judge agreed with the jury in 38 cases and 3 cases were referred to the High Court, of the two were acquitted and one was convicted.[77]

The system of trial with the aid of the Assessors did not prove a success although it was of great help to both the Judge and the accused. In 1875, 49 cases were tried with the aid of the Assessors of which the Judge agreed with the Assessors in 44 cases.[78] In 1901-02, 252 cases were tried with the aid of Assessors—the Judges concurred with the findings of both the Assessors in 27 cases and with one of the Assessors in 18 cases while in others that he did not agree with both.[79] In 1911-12, the Judges concurred with both the Assessors in 24 cases with one Assessor in 51 cases while in 46 cases he disagreed upto with.

Before 1906 persons called for acting as Jurors or Assessors were paid in the Assam Valley an allowance and travel expenditure by appropriate class provided they travelled for more than five miles. But those who came from within five miles did not receive any allowance. As a result, an eminent Jurist of the town found it an unnecessary burden to act as Juror in the local court. But from 1906, all persons were paid travelling and daily allowance irrespective of distance.[82] In the Surma Valley, of course, the Assessors were paid a daily allowance of Rs. 5 and reasonable expenses for travel since 1868.[83]

The system of jury which operated in the Assam Valley so successfully was not in force in the Surma Valley. Kamini Kumar Chanda, the first member of the Chief Commissioner's

Legislative Council from Sylhet moved a resolution suggesting its introduction in the Surma Valley also. But the local officers were not in favour of the proposal. Cosgrave, the Deputy Commissioner of Sylhet opined that the litigious[84] spirit of the people of the locality did not warrant its introduction there.[85] The jury system, however, was not introduced in the Surma Valley districts during our period.

Criminal cases were usually investigated by Police Officers and at each court there was a prosecuting Police Officers whose duty was to make a charge and prove the guilt of the accused persons.[86] People engaged lawyers to defend themselves, they thought if they had not the assistance of lawyer, they would not be heard. If the case was against the administration, Public Prosecutor was engaged to defend the case.[87] In case, an accused of a serious crime, particularly of murder, could not engage a counsel because of pecuniary circumstances, the Public Prosecutor might be required to act on his behalf.[88] Again, Government employed pleaders to defend the administration and the Government pleaders were declared as ex-officio Public Prosecutors under section 492 of Criminal Procedure Code, 1898.[89]

Justice in the hills

The Jurisdiction of the High Court of Calcutta was excluded from the Hill districts of Assam except over the European subjects of Crown. These districts and North Cachar Sub-Division of Mikir Hills district, along with certain Frontier tracts were administered under special rules originally drawn up under Act XXII of 1869 which removed the Garo Hills, Khasi and Jaintia Hills and Naga Hills from the jurisdiction of the High Court.[90] Subsequently these rules were reissued under the Schedules District Act in 1874. Further, the Frontier Tract Regulation of 1880 excluded these districts from the operation of the enactments relating to original procedure Code, the Civil Procedure Code was never introduced in the hills.[91]

The Scheduled District Act of 1874 provided for a similar system of civil and criminal administration in the hills. By these rules the Chief Commissioner was the Chief appellate authority in civil and criminal cases.[92] In criminal cases, reference could be made to the Chief Commissioner within a fixed time whereupon the latter might order for a retrial before him but in any case the decree ought to be issued by the Deputy Commissioner himself. The Chief Commissioner had no power to alter the sentence. The right of appeal was not conceded in the case of indigenous people. Outsiders were not denied the right of appeal. In criminal cases no appeal against the decision of the Deputy Commissioners could be taken to the Chief Commissioner unless punishment exceeded three years.[93]

The Deputy Commissioner in the Hill districts weilded considerable powers in both civil and criminal cases. The powers and functions of the District and Sessions Judge were vested in him. The Assistant Commissioners exercised powers and functions of Munsifs and Magistrates provided they were vested with these powers. No Assistant Commissioner could, however, be vested with more powers than that of a first class Magistrate.[94]

The Deputy Commissioners in the Hills could inflict any punishment including death, imprisonment for life provided in the Criminal Procedure Code. But punishment exceeding 7 years imprisonment and capital punishment required the approval of the Chief Commissioner. The only limitation in civil cases was that the fine imposed by the Deputy Commissioner ought not to exceed the amount of the value of the property of the person.[95]

The village tribunals presided over by village headmen chosen by the people tried all petty criminal and civil suits. Thus a Laskar in Garo Hills could try cases of theft, injury to property, injury to persons, not endangering life or limb, house tresspass and other minor crimes and could inflict punishment of fine upto Rs. 50 or could award restitution or compensation by distraint of property of the respondent. The procedure in the Court was simple. Cases were tried in open Durbar. Witnesses were examined under an oath. The proceedings were not recorded.[96] But the village tribunals had no jurisdiction over outsiders. An appeal from the village tribunal could be taken to the Assistant Commissioner.[97]

European British subjects

In 1872, Europeans were subject to the jurisdiction of the Muffasil courts but they could be tried by First Class Magistrates or by Judges of their own race. Before 1872, all cases involving Europeans had to be sent to the High Court in Calcutta. Further discrimination was made in regard to punishment between European and Indian subjects. The penalty imposed on European subjects was less than that of natives for similar offences. A First Class Magistrate could inflict only a sentence of three months imprisonment on a European subject whereas in the case of a native his competence extended upto two years. Similarly, the Sessions Court, which had full powers of sentence over natives, subject to confirmation by the High Court of Calcutta. Even death sentences, could pass only one year imprisonment on Europeans.[98]

In 1884, European British subjects could be tried by a Judge who was a Justice of the Peace. The powers of the Justice of the Peace were specially conferred on First Class Magistrates who were Europeans. But District Magistrates and Sessions Judges were Justices of Peace ex-officio. As such, natives holding such posts could try European subjects. In such cases the accused could claim a jury of which not less than one half shall be either Europeans or Americans. Moreover, an European British subject could claim in certain cases the applications of English Habeas Corpus.[99]

Appeals

It is human to err and a Judge is no exception. Sometimes the decision of a Judge may be faulty or his knowledge of law defective. He may unconsciously be swayed by prejudice, obstinacy or passion. His conclusion may be at variance with facts. So there is scope for miscarriage of justice. The Anglo-Indian administration believed in these possibilities. So it provided for an appeal. Appeals are of two kinds, appeals on points of facts and appeals on points of law. Appeals could be taken on the ground that the sentence passed on the accused was to the facts established.[100] In criminal matters one appeal was usually allowed on questions of fact, including matters was usually allowed on questions of fact, including the character of sentence passed. Generally appeals were adjusted against evidence inflicted on the defendent but Government also was allowed to appeal against an acquittal to the High Court. Provision was also made for retrial where there had been a flagrant miscarriage of justice.[101]

Legal system

The legal system of the Ahom Kingdom was gradually replaced by the Civil and Criminal Courts even before 1874. Acts passed by the Imperial Legislative Council were gradually extended to Assam. Thus the Criminal Procedure Code, the Evidence Act, the Control Act, the Limitation Act, the Specific Relief Act, the Guardian and Ward Act and Provincial Insolvency Act were extended to systematrial the whole legal system. Yet the private law of the people was not touched.[102] Thus the Succession Act was not to apply any Hindu, Buddhist or Muhammadan, though by special enactment it might be applied to certain cases. The Negotiable Instrument Act was not to apply to instruments in Oriental languages. Hindus retained their family laws regulating marriage, adoption, joint family, partition and inheritance. Muhammadans preserved their law of marriage of testamentary and intestate succession, and of religious endowments. In regard to rent and land tenure, Indian principles were mixed up with English doctrines.[103] The tribal customary laws were left untouched. The native Christians who could invoke neither customary laws in tribal areas nor native laws in plain areas, had to be dealt with separately.

Defects in the judiciary

The Judges of the Muffasil courts were drawn from Indian Civil Service whose main duty was executive. They had little experience in the administration of criminal law. The District and Sessions Judges were mainly Europeans. They were drawn from the same source, the Civil Service and it was commonly held that they were not the pick of the Civil Service.

The District Magistrate primarilly an executive officer and collector of revenue, was intimately associated with the repression of crime. He could direct the arrest of a suspected criminal and then could try him himself or cause him to be tried by some particular Magistrate. The Magistrates in his jurisdiction were not only under his control but were also his executive subordinates. Their advancements depended on his recommendation. Further he heard appeals against their decisions. Finally, he could bring cases to the notice of the Government or the High Court for reconsideration of sentence already passed. District Judge could return to the Executive line.[105] The District

Judges were subordinate to the Local Government and hence their promotion rested with it. Thus the machinery devised for their administration of justice was neither satisfactory nor efficient.

REFERENCES

1. Misra, B.B. : *The Central Administration of the East India Company* p. 298.
2. Barpuzari, H.K.: *Assam in the Days of the Company*, p. 28.
3. Ibid., p. 30.
4. Hamilton, E.: *An Account of Assam*, p. 49.
5. Ibid., p. 49.
6. Gohain, U.: *Assam Under the Ahoms*, p. 143.
7. Ibid., p. 143.
8. Barpuzari, H.K. : *Assam in the Days of the Company*, pp. 28-29.
9. Ibid., p. 30-32.
10. Ibid., p. 29.
11. Ibid., p. 29.
12. RAA 1874-76, para 110.
13. Ibid., para 111.
14. Ibid., para, 112.
15. Barpuzari, H.K.: *Assam in the Days of the Company*, pp. 191-192.
16. Ibid., p. 191.
17. Ibid., p. 192.
18. Assam Gazatteer, part IB, 27 June, 1874.
19. Ibid.
20. RAA 1874-76, part IIA, para 112.
21. Ibid., para 114.
22. Ibid., 1920-21, part II, para 77.
23. Ibid., para 77.
24. Ibid., 1874-76.
25. Ibid., para 130.
26. Ibid., 1874-76, part IIB, para 130.
27. Ibid., para 130.
28. Ibid., para 129.
29. Ibid., para 129.
30. Ibid.
31. Ibid.
32. Ibid., para 14.
33. RAEB, 1905-06, part II, para 136.
34. Ibid.
35. Ibid., para 136.
36. RAA 1874-76, part HB, para 326.
37. Ibid., para 327/68A, Assam Gazattee, Saturday, Nov. 188 .

38. RAA 1892-93, part IIB, para 114.
39. Ibid., 1901-02, part II, para 271.
40. Ibid., 1911-12, part II, para 244.
41. Ibid., 1920-21, part II, para 85.
42. Assam Gazattee, Saturday, Nov. 1882.
43. Ibid., November, 1882.
44. Ibid.
45. RAA 1892-93, part IIB, para 114.
46. Ibid., 1901-02, part II, para 272.
47. Assam Gazattee, Saturday, November, 1882.
48. RAA 1892-93, part II, para 118.
49. Ibid., 1901-02, part II, para 278.
50. Ibid., 1920-21, part II, para 90.
51. Ibid..
52. Ibid, para 84.
53. RAA 1874-76, part IIB, para 228.
54. Ibid.
55. Ibid., para 229.
56. RAEBA 1905-06, part II, para 135.
57. Imperial Gazatte, Vol. IV, p. 148.
58. RAEBA 1905-06, part II, para 135.
59. RAA 1874-76, part IIB, para 242.
60. Ibid., para 242.
61. RAEBA, 1905-06. part II, para 135.
62. Assam Gazattee, Saturday, November, 1882.
63. RAA 1892-93, part IIA para 88.
64. Ibid., 1901-02, part II, para 229.
65. Ibid., 1911-12, part II, para 224.
66. Ibid., 1920-21, part II, para 65.
67. Assam Gozattee, Saturday, November, 1882.
68. Ibid.
69. RAA 1892-93, part II, para 100.
70. Ibid., 1901-92, part II, para 256.
71. Assam Gazattee, Saturday, November, 1882.
72. RAA 1892-93, part II, para 95.
73. PGAJD, No. 1 of 1912.
74. Ibid., No. 64 and No. 86 of 1920.
75. Ibid., No. 86 of 1920.
76. RAA 1874-76, part IIB, para 242.
77. Ibid., 1911-12, part II, para 25.
78. Ibid., 1874-76, part IIB, para 242.
79. Ibid., 1901-02, part II, para 246.
80. Ibid., 1911-12, part II, para 255.
81. PGAJD No. 1 of 1920.
82. Ibid.
83. Ibid., No. 4 of 1920.
84. Ibid.,No. 1 of 1914.

85. PGAJD No. 12 of 1914
86. Ibid., No. 31 of 1916.
87. Ibid., No. 31 of 1916.
88. Ibid., No. 35 of 1918.
89. Ibid., No. 11 of 1918.
90. RAA 1882-83, part II, para 103.
91. Ibid.
92. Imperial Gazatte, Vol. IV, p. 84.
93. Assam Gazattee, part IB, Saturday, 1874.
94. Ibid.
95. Assam Gazattee, Part IB, Saturday, January, 1874.
96. RAA 1872-83, part II, para 103.
97. Assam Gazattee, Part IB, Saturday, January, 1874.
98. Sharma, S.R.: *Evolution of Public Administration in India*, p. 235.
99. Ibid., pp. 235-36.
100. Ibid., p. 231.
101. Ibid., p. 231.
102. Keith, A.B.: *A Constitutional History of India*, p. 210.
103. Ibid., p. 210-11.
104. Sharma, S.R.: *Evolution of Public Administration in India*, p. 237.
105. Ibid. p. 237.

7

ADMINISTRATION OF POLICE

THE maintenance of law and order in the State is one of the essential functions of a modern Government. The agency through which the State operates for this purpose is Police. If the administration of police is efficient and force adequate, the life and property of the individual are Secure and the State prospers because national wealth will increase. Inefficiency and inadequacy of the police force will lead to chaos and disorder. The individual will have no incentive to save capital without which no nation can progress. Therefore, the administration of police is very important.

Police functions during the Ahom age

The administration of police by the provincial Government was in a sense a new thing in Assams. Law and order was a local responsibility under the Ahoms. Therefore, during the Ahom rule, there was no organised police force. Whenever there was a breach of peace, the officers of the King who were essentially military and civil officers took cognizance of it and punished the offenders.[1] In each village, however, there was a Gaonbura who was the recognised head of the village and who adjudicated all petty disputes. There was no village watchman or any police officer for the detection and prevention of crime. Nor was there any State organization of police for this purpose.

Police organization upto 1874

The British came to Assam at a time when law and order had completely collapsed under the pressure of internal rebellion and external aggression.[2] It was their primary obligation as rulers of the new territory to provide peace and security. Therefore, immediately after the annexation of Assam the province was put under Martial Law which effected an improvement in the situation.

During the period when the country was under Martial Law (1824-1828) the predatory hordes were frightened and were compelled to remain quiet. The highwaymen, robbers and burglars and other peace disturbing elements were suppressed. But when Martial Law was withdrawn, Mr. David Scott who was entrusted with the responsibility for the maintenance of law and order did not wish to bring into existence an organization which was costly and cumbersome. He, therefore, revived the indigenous institutions for police purposes.[3] Of course, for the suppression of violent disturbances a police force was created. In each district and in some strategic parts of the province, some Police Stations were established and put under a Daroga or Thanedar, with a Jamadar, Mohurrer and a few Barkandaz. The revenue officers of the localities entitled Chaudhuries, Patgiris and Mouzadars were also instructed to help him. To deal with major disturbance a military force used to be despatched and a poll tax was realised from the people of the locality for its maintenance.[4] In 1837, regulation of 1817 was applied to Assam for police administration.[5]

After the Police Commission's recommendations were received and Police Act of 1861 was passed provisions of the Police Act of 1861 were extended to Assam.[6] The entire police force of Assam was put under the charge of the Inspector General of Police, Bengal, and the Deputy Commissioners of Assam districts were provided with an Assistant to help him in the administration of police.

Administration of police under the chief commissioners

When Assam was constituted into a Chief Commissionership the police force of the province was brought under a general Police District under the Police Act of 1861.[7] But no separate officer was appointed as Inspector General of Police. The Chief Commissioner himself was the Inspector General of Police.[8] The first Chief Commissioner Keatings, himself was not in favour of any separate officers to control the police force, instead he wanted an Assistant Secretary of Assistant Commissioner's to help him in the administration of police.[9] The inspection of a force spread over such a vast and wild region as Assam, was well neigh impossible for a single person. Therefore, it became difficult for the Chief Commissioner to bestow adequate attention to police administration which consisted of not only Civil and Armed forces of the Province but Military and Rural Police as well. So in 1876 a separate officer was appointed to relieve the Chief Commissioner of Assam from his duties as Inspector General of Police.[10] The Inspector General of Police was held responsible not only for the maintenance of law and order in the police, he was also entrusted with subjects like the administration of Jail, Excise and Stamps.

Section 4 of the Police Act of 1861 vested the administration of police in Assam in the Inspector General of Police and such number of Deputy Inspectors General or Assistant Inspectors General as the Local Goverment might appoint.[11] But as the police force in Assam was small compared to other provinces, no deputy or assistant was appointed to help the Inspector General. However, the Inspector General was vested with the full powers of a Magistrate throughout the province.[12] Those powers, of course, were to be exercised for the preservation of peace, prevention or detection of crime, or apprehension or detection of offenders, in the absence of a Magistrate.[13] The Inspector General had complete control over the entire police force of the province and subject to the approval of the Local Government, he framed such rules and passed orders for the forces as he thought fit.[14]

The police force of Assam consisted of Civil Police, Armed Police, Military Police, River and Railway Police and Rural Police and Chaukidari Police in the districts of Sylhet and Goalpara. The Civil Police was ordinarily responsible for the maintenance of law and order, prevention and detection of crime and criminals.[15] At the headquarters of each district a reserve of armed force was maintained for providing escort, and such duty as the suppression of disturbances and to meet any emergency.[16] The Railway Police were engaged for the prevention of crime in Railways. The River Police were employed for the haors or beels in Sylhet. In Goalpara district, Panchayats employed for watch and ward purpose Chowkidars in the villages. In some cases Union Police were employed in towns for watch and ward purposes.[18]

For the purpose of police administration the whole province was divided into districts and the police of the district was placed under a Superintendent of Police. The district was again divided into Sub-Divisions and placed them under an Assistant or Deputy Superintendent of Police and the Sub-Division was again divided into Circles placed them under Inspectors. The Circle was divided into Stations and placed them under Sub-Inspectors. A Station might have Outposts and Beats in towns. In 1874, there were 53 Stations and 48 Outposts in Assam.[19] In 1920 in all the twelve Districts of Assam there were 114 Police Stations and 10 Outposts.

The maintenance of Law and Order in the district was the responsibility of the Deputy Commissioner and as such the police force in a district was under the general control and direction of the Deputy Commisioner. But the administration was vested in the District Superintendent of Police. The Deputy Commissioner had no authority to interfere in the internal organisation or discipline of the force. The Superintendent of Police was free to effect internal economy in the force or in purely departmental affairs. But even in such matters the Superintendent was bound to pay due regard to the wishes and suggestions of the Deputy Commissioner. In case of difference of opinion regarding police adminstration, it was the obligation of the Superintendent to carry out the orders of the Deputy Commissioner but he could request him to refer the point under dispute to the Commissioner so far as the Assam Valley districts was concerned and the Inspector General so far as the Hill districts and Surma Valley districts were concerned. Any District Superintendent of Police who by passed unjustly the instructions and orders of the Deputy Commissioner was subject to disciplinary punishments.[21] The Deputy Commissioner maintained the confidential records of the District Superintendent of Police. The relation between the Sub-Divisional Officer and the Sub-Divisional Police Officer stood on the same footing as between the Deputy Commissioner and the Superintendent of Police.[22]

The actual work of maintenance of law and order, the prevention and detection of crime, the arrest of criminals was the function of the Stations. Station was usually placed in charge of a Sub-Inspector who was assisted by one or more Assistant Inspectors, Moherrier and some Constables. Criminal Procedure Code divided offences into cognizable and non-cognizable. The police dealt with cognizable crimes. It was the duty of the Officer-in-Charge of the Police Station to proceed to the spot, to investigate serious cases. He entered into his diary the statement of person he examined; or he could search the residence of employed persons for the recovery of stolen property, and record confessions before a Magistrate. If crime was detected, he had to take the accused person to the Magistrate under arrest or could be committed to sessions if it was serious crime. But no man could be detained for more than 24 hours without the orders of a Magistrate. If no evidence was found or if the case was proved to be a false one, the Magistrate recorded it and dismissed the case. Persons responsible for reporting false cases could be prosecuted. Cases of minor importance could be investigated by the Head Constable or by Literate Constables.[23]

The preventive measures of a Police Station were not less important. Each station had a register of habitual offenders, suspected bad characters and convicts. The police force maintained regular watch over their activities. Any change of their address was correctly recorded and their movements in the night was closely watched. Special watch was maintained over heinous criminals, particularly over those who were released under mark system. Sometimes they were required to furnish security for good behaviour or otherwise imprisoned in default.[24]

Besides Police Stations there were some Outposts within the jurisdiction of a Police Station. They were of two categories. First, Independent Outposts which though within the jurisdiction of the Police Stations and attached to it reported crime directly to the Sub-District Police Officer and maintained a register of cases. In a sense it was a minor Police Station. Second, the Subordinate Outposts which reported crime through the Police Station within whose jurisdiction it was situated. If a Police Station was situated within a town area was sub-divided into a number of Beats and Outposts for police purposes. Though regular police was employed for watch and ward purpose, in towns declared as "unions". Watchmen were employed by the union authority for watch and ward purpose.[25]

Besides the prevention and detection of crime, the police, under Section 30 of the Police Act of 1861 was given the power to regulate public assemblies, processions, ceremonies and festivals in public places.[26] Section 31 of the same Act authorised the police to keep order on public roads, Ghats and landing places and all other places of public resort and prevent obstructions to assemblies and processions.[27] Any person who on any road or in any open place or street or thorough fare within the limits of any town to which Section 34 of the Act was extended, committed any offence convening obstruction, inconvenience, annoyance risk, danger, or damage of the resident, or passengers, might be prosecuted. For the proper discharge of the duties under this Section, the police was given power to arrest any person without a warrant.[28] Drunkards, people throwing filth on the streets, or keeping dangerous places like tank, well or reservoir and even hawkers on the streets and people parking carts unnecessarily for a long time on roads were taken into custody.[29] This Section also aimed at the prevention of cruelty to animals. Under it, the police had the power to arrest any person who wantonly or cruelly beat, drove or abused any animal. At the same time it forced people to correct their sense of decency as it also empowered the police to see any person who wilfully or indecently exposed his person or any offensive deformity or disease or committed nuisance by easing himself or by bathing or washing in any tank or reservoir not being a place set apart for that purpose.[30] A large number of policemen were employed particularly in the towns for the enforcement of these regulations. At every important road crossings and busy roads, at every market place or hats in the rural areas policemen were stationed during busy hours and festival seasons.[31]

Another aspect of Civil Police administration was the maintenance and supervision of cattle pouds.[32] A considerable number of men were engaged in the Assam Valley for this purpose. The ponds within a District was under the immediate management and supervision of the District Superintendent of Police subject to the general control of the Deputy Commissioner.[33] The ponds were usually kept in charge of a Literate

Constable. He had to maintain a register showing the cattle put in the ponds and released therefrom. He had to arrange the feeding of the cattle in the pounds. Sometimes the ponds were kept in charge of a postmaster or a school teacher or a special keeper. In these cases the station officer had the responsibility to see that fodder and water was properly supplied. He also examined and checked the register of ponds.[34]

River police

For the prevention of crime and maintenance of law and order in the beels or haors of Sylhet, Ghats, hats or on river banks and boat stopping places in Goalpara, river patrol police force was created.[35] In 1915 a separate River Police District was created in Sylhet. It had a force consisting of Sub-Inspectors, two Head constables and nineteen Constables, one Inspector and Head constables and Constables were added.[36] The Superintendent of Police, Sylhet, was the ex-officio Superintendent of River Police. The duty of River Police was mainly preventive in character. Usually a Sub-Inspector in charge of a party of a circle, patrolled along the regular trade routes and routes between two or more villages paying special attention to all known and bad suspected characters day and night, specially in the night.[37] As a result of constant patrolling crime in the river bed declined.

Railway police

Railway Police was employed in the Assam Bengal Railway and Jorhat State Railway. The cost of the force was borne by the Railway authorities.[38] But the administration of the police was in the hands of the Inspector General of Police.[39] The watch and ward duties were performed by Railway personnel; the duty of the Railway Police was to prevent crime by patrolling in the trains. The Policemen used to travel in plain clothes and watched the movements of suspected characters and arrested, if necessary, the persons who violated the Railway regulations or committed crime.[40]

Municipal and rural police

Besides the regular police, there was the Municipal Police in the towns which were constituted into "Unions" under the

Bengal Municipal Act, 1876.[41] The work of the watch and ward was performed by the police in the towns. In theory they were night watchmen but in practice they had certain amount of day duty as well.[42]

Rural Police was employed in Sylhet and Cachar districts of the Surma Valley and in the Goalpara district in the Assam Valley.[43] The village police was regulated by the Chowkidari Act of 1870 in Goalpara and in Sylhet their services were governed by the Regulation XX of 1817.[44] In Cachar their appointment and remuneration was regulated by the Local Customs. In 1833 a Regulation (Regulation 1 of 1833) was passed and these placed the Chowkidari organization on a better footing in the Surma Valley districts.[45] This Regulation provided for the creation of village police circles and beats, for the appointment of village police thereto, for the recovery of their pay, for the accurate definition of their duties and enforcement.

The principal duty of the village police was to observe the movements of bad characters and inform the officer anything that might affect the peace and tranquility of the locality.[46] But he was required to report all serious crime to the police officer in charge of the Police Station of the village and to arrest persons against whom warrant was issued or who were charged with cognizable offences.[47] The service of the village police was utilised for the collection of vital statistics as well.[48]

In the Assam Valley except in Goalpara where there was Rural Police, law and order in villages was managed by Goanbura or village elder. He was recognised as the representative of the village and gave relevant information to the police.[49] He was not paid any remuneration for a long time, but he was given rent free land and a Sanad.[50] Though he was required to report breach of peace to police he was not under any police authority. His responsibility was to the Magistrate of his area. Besides him, the Mouzadars and Mandals were also required to give information and assist the police officers in the prevention and detection of crime.[51]

Military police

In a State like Assam the story of the administration of police is hardly complete without a reference to Military Police. The economic growth of Assam was threatened with a peculiar danger of transfrontier forays. The frontiers were infested with wild tribes who regarded raids on the plains as acts of valour. The most effective method of dealing with them was relatiatory expeditions into the tribal territory. For such small expeditions the employment of regular military force would have been costly while it was beyond the capacity of the armed civil police to deal with them.[52] The task of pacifying and surrounding these wild hordes was entrusted to the Military Police under the command of the civil authority.

After Martial Law was withdrawn in 1828, regular British soldiers were also withdrawn from Assam leaving the defence of the valley to Rangpore Light Infantry now named Assam Light Infantry after serving three years in Assam, and Surma Valley to Sylhet Light Infantry.[53] Another battalion of Sebundy corps was raised in 1835 to defend the Sadiya frontier. This was converted into Second Assam Light Infantry in 1842.[54] But the defence of the frontiers against the tribal incursions required more soldiers than the two corps could provide and to meet the situation Semi-military force under civil Government had to be organised. As early as 1835 a force known as Cachar Levy recruited mainly from Rabhas, Cacharies and kindened tribes was raised and in 1840 another force was recruited under the name of Jorhat Militia.[55] They guarded the eastern frontier posts from Kamrup to Sibsagar supported by regular troops behind at Nowgong and Silchar.

But the employment of Semi-military Sebundy troops under Civil Police to guard eastern frontier between Kamrup and Rangpore and Assam Light Infantry for others north of the Brahmaputra proved inexpedient. Therefore in March 1873 Bengal Government had deputed one officer Mr. Barker to report for reorganisation of North East Frontier Police; in June he recommended the division of police in the frontier districts into Civil and Frontier forces.[56] Assam being separated in 1874 the Chief Commissioner was requested to make a proposal for the reorganisation. The Chief Commissioner, therefore, proposed as early in 1875 the organisation of Military Police disbanding the Cachar Levy and Jorhat Militia for the frontiers of Assam with men to be recruited from Jalpaiguri.[57] In 1878, Military Police were formed into a separate force of 5 battalions and one detachment of it was maintained in each district. It performed quasi-military duties in guarding the Frontier Out-posts and providing guards, escorts and other semi-civil duties at head-quarters of districts and sub-divisions. Besides, it was held as garrisons in the wild districts of Garo Hills, Naga Hills and Lushai Hills. The organization of this force resulted in the reduction of the strength of the armed Civil Police in Assam.[58]

In 1882, Sir Charles Elliot again proposed the reorganization of Frontier Police.[59] As a part of the scheme the Frontier Police was now formed into a essentially Military body and separate from the Civil Police. Its members were drilled and equipped as soldiers, bore Military designations and were organised for service as an armed force. The Frontier Police was divided into four battalions for Lakhimpur district, Naga Hills district, Garo district and the Surma valley, besides two detachments were employed on the frontier defence of Sibsagar and Darrang.[60] The battalions were put under the command of European Commander general three of whom were Military officers lent to the Chief Commissioner for five years and one was a civilian of Bengal Police service selected for the post for his special qualifications and previous service in a Military capacity.[61]

The Military Police force was orginally regulated by the Police Act of 1861.[62] A mixed staff of Military and Civil Police officers of the Bengal list assisted the Inspector General in its administration. But in 1882 Assam Frontier Police Regulation was passed to provide for the enforcement of discipline and assimilate the terms of service to those prevailing in the Native Army.[63] Subsequently in 1890 and in 1912 the conditions were further modified. But police appellation seems to have been unpopular among the Servicemen and as such to give more prestige to the force and raise the status and esprit de corps of the officer and men, the designation of the Force was changed to Assam Rifles.[64] A new Act known as Assam Rifles Act was passed to govern their services without altering their status as a Civil force.[65]

Civil administration by police officers

The police officers in Assam were not only employed for the maintenance of law and order, in some instances they were engaged in civil administration and political duties. In the hill areas instead of Civil Officers, Police Officers were put in charge of general administration. The Sub-Divisional Officers of North Cachar and Wokha Sub-Divisions were Assistant Superintendent of Police.[66] The Political Officer at Sadiya was also an Assistant Superintendent of Police.[67] Besides the police officers were made ex-officio Assistant Inspectors of Factories and tea gardens of the province.[68] The Military Police Commandants were either Eurasians or Europeans. Therefore, Assam required a good number of European or Eurasian police officers who should have been well-versed in the peculiar conditions of the province and served there for longer time. But Assam did not have a separate police service of its own, it borrowed its officers from the Bengal administration.[69]

Mode of recruitment of police officers

The police administration in Assam thus suffered from one grave defect, that it depended always for its officers on the Bengal Government who lent the services of its officers usually for 5 years. It was quite natural that Bengal offered second rate men for service in Assam. Added to this was the climate of Assam. The means of communication induced very few efficient officers to volunteer their services to this province. Again after the officers gained adequate experience of the local conditions they were recalled to Bengal. Very few opted to stay in Assam, majority reverted to their original province. To mitigate this evil, Sir Charles Elliot proposed the amalgamation of the Provincial Civil Service and the Police Service. In other words, he desired the combination of civil and police functions in one and the same hands. The Assistant and Extra Assistant Commissioners of the province should be entrusted with police functions.[70] The proposal was negatived by the Government of India who considered that there should be separate police officers[71] for watch and ward in the plain districts of Assam. In 1902 when police service was reorganised Assam police was separated from Bengal cadre. While Indian Police Service officers were recruited for Assam by examination in England the Deputy and Assistant Superintendents were recruited from the provincial service.[72]

In the civil branch of subordinate service and in the rank and file, no technical qualification was necessary for employment. But educated people were reluctant to take up service in the police department as the salary was not attractive nor was the prospect of promotion bright.[73] In 1874, the salary of a constable was Rs. 6 per month less than that of an agricultural labour.[74] In 1896, a Head constable was drawing Rs. 9 per month.[75]

After the reorganization of the police department the reversion of the experienced police officers to their parent posts in Bengal was ended. But the police officers still suffered from a sense of injustice. The superior posts in the service was not open to the personnel of their branch. The Inspector General of Police was always a member of Indian Civil Service.[76] The police officers remained under the civil officers who recommended for their promotion and reported on their services.[77]

Efficiency and discipline in the force

Fortunately for Assam there was practically no serious crime in the Assam Valley. Professional criminals were almost absent habitual crime was a rare thing.[78] Of course this was not due to the efficiency of the administration of police. It must be attributed to the character of the people.

At the beginning of our period the discipline in the police was on the whole good though its salary was less than that of rural labourer and the rate of illiteracy among policemen was very high. The percentage of punishment of police personnel was 20.08 and 3.14 by the judicial in 1874.[79] In 1891, we find the same state of affairs.[80] Even though there was no increase in literacy or in salary of the police personnel.

The total strength of the police force in 1874 was 3,352.[81] In 1903-04 they did not change considerably. We find 384 officers and 2,289 men in 1903-04, thus there was one policeman for every 2185 men with 20 square miles area.[82]

After the reorganisation of the subordinate services the strength of the police force rose from 3,160 into 3,226 in 1912.[83] But there was a slight increase in the percentage of punishment, both departmental and judicial because of high standard of discipline enforced upon the force. The strength of civil police force did not increase significantly. Even in 1918 it was 3,633.[84]

The population of the province had by this time increased considerably and as such the number of cases dealt with by the police also increased. But the increase in the number of cases was due to the increase in population than to criminal habit of the people. The number of cases reported was 12,856[85] in 1881, 11,743[86] in 1892-93, 16,180[87] in 1911-12 but in 1919 it was 18,014.[88] The rise in the number of cases in 1911-12 and in 1919 was largely due to immigration and rising prices.[89]

The administration of police in Assam was thus on the whole satisfactory. The police succeeded in maintaining law and order though they failed in the detection of house breaking and theft cases.[90] Serious oppression by the police was not a common thing but petty exactions were not uncommon.[91] The moral tone of the policemen, however, improved after the Subordinate Services were recognised and literacy increased among the policemen.

The administration of police in Assam during the period was on the whole satisfactory. The police on the whole was successful in maintaining law and order though it was not completely successful in the defeation of crime—particularly of house breaking and theft cases. Further police administration was not oppressive and tyrannical, though petty exactions from the innocent was not uncommon. The level of administration improved considerably after the reorganization of the service in 1901. But there was no increase in the strength of the force even though there was increase in population. There was one policeman per population which was much less to the standard fixed by the Police Commission.

REFERENCES

1. Gohain, U.N.: *Assam Under the Ahoms*, p. 143.
2. Barpuzari, H.K.: *Assam in the Days of the Company*, p. 12.
3. Ibid., p. 32.
4. Ibid., p. 32.
5. Idid.
6. RAA 1874-76, part IIA, para 112.
7. RAA, 1920, part II, para 105.
8. PGIHJUD No. 411 of April, 1874.
9. PGIHEST No. 98 of August, 1876.

10. PGIHEST No. 98 of August, 1876.
11. Police Act, 1861, Sec. 3.
12. Ibid., Sec. 3.
13. Assam Police Manual, part I, Rule 5.
14. Ibid., Sec. 3.
15. Imperial Gazatteer, Vol. IV, p. 388.
16. Ibid, p. 389.
17. PGAJD No. 17-18 of February, 1918.
18. RAA 1892-93, part IIA, para 110.
19. RAA 1874-75, part IIA, para 54.
20. RAA 1920-21, part II, para 146.
21. Assam Police Manual, part I, Rule 25.
22. Ibid., Rule 27.
23. Imperial Gazatteer, Vol. IV, p. 392-93.
24. Ibid., p. 393.
25. RAA 1892-93, part IIA, para 110.
26. Police Act of 1861, Sec. 30.
27. Ibid, Sec. 31.
28. Ibid.
29. Ibid., Sec. 34.
30. Ibid Sec. 44.
31. Ibid., Sec. 31.
32. Report of the Provincial Police Committee 1902, para 33.
33. Assam Police Manual, part V, Rule 105.
34. Ibid., Rule 105.
35. PGAJD No. 17 & 18 of February, 1918.
36. Ibid., No. 39 of April, 1915.
37. Ibid., No. 17 of February, 1918.
38. Report of the Provincial Police Committee 1902, para 37.
39. Ibid, para 37.
40. PGAJD No. 3 of August, 1912.
41. RAA 1892-93, part IIA, para 110.
42. RAEBA, 1905-06, part II, para 127.
43. RAA 1882-83, part II, para 105.
44. Ibid.
45. Ibid.
46. Imperial Gazatteer, Vol. VI, p. 392.
47. Ibid., p. 392.
48. Ibid.
49. PGARD No. 160 of November 1904.
50. Ibid.
51. Ibid.
52. Shakespear: *History of Assam Rifles*, p. V.
53. Bhuyan, S.K.: Anglo-Assamese Relations, p. 555.
54. Ibid.
55. Ibid.
56. PGIHPD Nos. 23-37 of March, 1876.

57. PGIHPD Nos. 23-37 of March, 1876.
58. Imperial Gazatteer, Vol. VI, p. 101.
59. PGIHPD No. 86 of August, 1883.
60. Ibid., No. 11 of December, 1884.
61. Ibid.
62. RAR 1882-83, part IIA, para 105.
63. Ibid.
64. PGAJD No. 53-54, 1917.
65. Ibid., No. 54, 1917.
66. Ibid., No. 2 of September, 1878.
67. Ibid.
68. PGIHPD No. 18 of April, 1888.
69. Ibid., No. 4 of December, 1875.
70. Ibid., No. 33-37 of March, 1878.
71. Ibid., No. 20-21, June, 1878.
72. Assam Police Manual, part I, Rule 20.
73. Imperial Gazatteer, Vol. VI, p. 100.
74. RAP 1874, para 21.
75. Report of the Provincial Police Committee, 1902, para 15.
76. Assam Police Manual, part I, Rule 20.
77. Report of the Provincial Police Committee, 1902, para 35.
78. RAR 1874, para 7.
79. Ibid., para 27.
80. Ibid., para 47.
81. RAP 1874, para 6.
82. Imperial Gazatteer, Vol. VI, p. 99
83. RAP 1911-12, para 231.
84. Ibid., 1919, para 10.
85. ROAPA 1881, para 12.
86. RAA 1892-93, part IIA, para 76.
87. Ibid., 1911-12, part II, para 339.
88. Ibid., 1920-21, part I, para 5.
89. Ibid., 1918-19, part II, Cp. III, Sec. 3.
90. Report of the Provincial Police Committee, 1902, para 22.
91. Ibid., para 36.

8

CONCLUSION

THE history of the Development of Administration of Assam is not only fascinating but also instructive. The East India Company was formed in 1600 to trade and commerce with the India which was a land of fabulous wealth. Instead of concerning themselves with commercial articles in course of their trade and commerce, disintegrating political condition encouraged the Company to take up the trade in arms and warfare which was much more paying than the legitimate profits of trade. In course of their participation in the indigenous warfare they were further lured by the prospect of founding an Empire in India. In course of time they succeeded in establishing it. But the essential motive behind the Indian empire was to exploit the resources of India, as neither climate, nor the people or its culture had any attraction to the British adventures who understood very little of them. As the Empire became a reality the administration of the country was geared up to facilitate the systematic exploitation for as long a time as it could be.

The British penetration into Assam began at a time when unfortunately the kingdom of the Ahoms reached the nadir of its decadence and no longer capable of restoring peace and order in the Kingdom. The outlying provincial administrators ceased to obey the commands of their royal master. The Burmese took advantage of internal feuds and tried to establish their hegemony over their Mongoloid neighbour. The British were busy in suppressing the Marathas and the predatory hoards which were still powerful. But as soon as they settled their accounts with them, they came to secure the North East Frontier as Bengal was the nerve centre of the English Empire in India.

The British relations with Assam had long before begun and they had already collected valuable information regarding the province much ahead of actual operations. They had once helped the Ahom Prince to suppress rebellion at a critical time in 1793-94. The outbreak of the Ahom-Burmese hostilities provided an opportunity to annex Assam thus pushing the North East Frontier to their natural boundaries.

The Ahom prince had sought the British help to push back the Tibeto-Burmans. But at the end of hostilities the British occupied Assam, and held it. The Central Administration of the Company did not like to assume the entire territory under its immediate management as they were not sure of its outcome. Only on an experimental basis Lower Assam was added to the charge of Mr. David Scott who had an intimate knowledge of the land from his services in the administration of the North East Frontier of the British India. In the rest the indigenous princes and their system of administration were maintained.

First Lower Assam up to Bisvanath including the three thanas of Goalpara, Dhubri and Karaibari transferred from Bengal in 1825 were divided into four districts of Kamrup, Goalpara, Nowgong and Tezpur in 1832. Next when Upper Assam was annexed in 1838, two districts of Lakhimpur and Sibsagar were created. Khasiand Jaintia Hills were made a district of Assam Commission. In 1835 Sadiya and in 1842 Matak territories were added to Lakhimpur district. The headquarter was transfered to Dibrugarh in the Matak country. The territories of Govinda Chandra was placed under a British Officer in 1832 after his death and Tularam's territories were added to it in 1853 when he was pensioned off. Garo Hills were separated from Cooch-Behar and added to the Goalpara district of Assam. In 1869 it was constituted into a separate district. Angami Naga Hills were formed into a district in 1866 and brought under direct administration. In 1875, Lhota Naga territory, 1889 Ao territory and in 1917 Luki tracts were annexed, to the district, the headquarters of which was transferred to Kohima in 1878. The Chin Lashai Hills of Bengal and Assam were united under single administrative unit in 1898 and placed under Assam Administration which had many other tribal areas of similar nature under its administration. Finally, Sylhet was transferred to Assam to make it a sizeable province and in 1874 the new province came into being.

Thus nearly three quarters of a century was required to consolidate the whole of Assam into a unit of administration. It is obvious that a province like Assam was too diversified and unweildy to be treated as one single and coherent unit. As such that symmetry and naturalness of division of the province which is expected of a unified conception are lacking in this province. The only factor that influenced and necessitated the division was administrative convenience. This spasmodic and irrational method of formation of the province had an interesting sequel. With the growth of education the different self-conscious communities have split themselves into political fagments. But this incongrous formation under a single administration had an advantage in a wider sense. It brought together under a single Government different races and communities and thus afforded opportunity to live together and understand each other which included broader national vision which was so urgent for a province like Assam.

The Administration of Assam was put in charge of a person who was Commissioner of the whole territory and Political Agent at the same time in frontier relations in 1826. The Commissioner, however, introduced a system of personal Government, rather than a formal regulated system. But in 1833 a system of codes was drawn up to guide the administrators in Assam Administration. But the hills which were inhabited by the wild tribes who presented a complex of social and political practices were still left unregulated. The Assam Code underwent further refinement in 1847, and finally replaced by the Civil Procedure Code in 1861 and Criminal Procedure Code in 1863. But these were only for the plains of the Brahamaputra Valley, not for the whole province. The hills remained outside the civil and criminal procedures of the British India.

When Assam was formed into a Chief Commissionership, the system of personal administration of the chief of the state was not materially affected. Rather the Chief Commissioner became the fountain of all powers and he guided practically the whole range of administration of the province. He was provided with assistants in the districts and no Head of any Department was there to help him at the headquarters save and except his Secretary and Assistant Secretary. Only jurisdiction of the High Court over the two valley districts was retained and he was relieved of appeliate jurisdiction in those districts.

The province, however, progressed steadily and with its development, the administrative machinery had to be elaborated to provide for the changed circumstances. Thus we see in 1877 an Inspector General of Police was appointed and further he was given charge of the departments of Excise Stamps and made the Registrar-General of the province. In 1880, the judge of the Assam Valley was vested ex-officio with the powers of a Commissioner of a division. Further the Commissioner was relieved of judicial duties when Commissioner of Excise was given charge of the same in 1903. To cope with the developed agriculture and settlement works a Director of Land Records was appointed and given the charge of agriculture to relieve the Chief Commissioner.

In the Secretariat of the Chief Commissioner, business had multiplied and no longer one Secretary and an Assistant sufficed. More Secretaries and Assistant Secretaries were provided. At the time when Reforms of 1919 were introduced we find no less than two Secretaries and a number of under Secretaries in the Secretariat of the Chief Commissioner.

Thus looking at the successive developments it appear that the chief of Assam Commission was vested with more and more powers to deal with the peculiar needs of the province. Its strategic importance, undeveloped potentialities, the preponderently tribal nature of its population required the personal care, initiative and unsophisticated system of administrative machinery to foster and grow the latent potentials. Therefore, it was separated from Bengal Government and put under Non-Regulated system of a Chief Commissioner. The Chief Commissioner was increasingly vested with administrative, executive and legislative powers. He was given the help of more responsible officers like the Heads of Administrative Departments, Divisional Commissioners and finally in recognition of the progress of the province, Legislative Council was set up. Under Government of India Act, 1919, it was made a Governor's province.

In the Administration of Land Revenue the British had acquired some experience from Bengal. They wanted to rectify the mistakes they had already committed elsewhere in India. So when they commuted the manual labour in favour of monetary payment they introduced ryotwary system of settlement with the people. Under the system they began to collect revenue directly from the cultivators of land, but utilised the indegenous institutions for the collection as far as it suited their purpose. Thus Choudhuries and Mouzadars were employed for the collection of revenue but not under regular employment as salaried servants but as commission agents who would take pains for collection. Settlement was made periodically thus retaining the future possibility of enhancement of demand. From 1870 we find them following a system of decennial settlement when tacitly the principle of hereditary succession to land was recognised but never the rent wasfixed as under permanent settlement. To accommodate the Ahom practices and thus allay the lay and temporal magnets provision was made for special revenue tenures. Thus Chamua, Khat, Six-pie Lakhiraj and Tentwenties in Sibsagar were provided. Besides these were Nisf Khiraj tenures for Brahmuttar and Dharmuttar lands were also provided. To increase revenue and bring more and more land under production special rules were provided for the Assam Valley. Wild lands could be taken up for cultivation and could be given up with due notice. People taking up fallow land enjoyed right to enjoy some benefits like exemption of revenue for some years and then revenue was imposed at a progressive rate. This helped the plantation industry in particular and attracted immigrants from outside the province.

In the hill districts where Jhum cultivation was practised by the tribes revenue was assessed in a different manner. A poll-tax was realised from each house through the village whip. In the permanently settled areas of Sylhet and Goalpara the revenue system was the same as in Bengal because agreement to that effect had already been arrived at before they were transferred to Assam.

For the administration of land revenue survey of land was essential. Survey of land of the new province beginning with cadastral system was systematised by the introduction of theodolite system. Duely surveyed land register was maintained and transfer of land was registered. Registry offices were set up althrough the province. Where land transaction was frequent Sub-Registrar's offices were set-up.

To invigorate the land revenue administration, to stimulate agriculture and proper maintenance of records a highly responsible officer of the rank of Assam Commission with the designation of Director of Agriculture aud Land Records was appointed as early as 1882. A separate revenue staff under a Sub-Deputy Collector was maintained at each sub-division. All executive officers of the Government had to possess a knowledge of the revenue system of the country and undertake the inspection of reveuue administration while on tour.

Thus, in prospective it appears that Land Revenue Administration in Assam had assumed its definite shape by 1920. Historically it owes its origin to the practices inherited from the decadent period of Ahom rule and changed slowly, not without mistakes, by the British who were alien to the country. They could, only with difficulty, by degrees appreciate the requirements and feelings of the people and evolve a system of administration suitable for them.

The Administration of Justice in Assam during the Chief Commissionership period (1874-1920) had many distinctive features of its own. But it was not altogether a new system created for Assam. After the withdrawal of Martial Law from Assam it was administered as a Non-Regulation province. The chaotic conditions and the less developed races in Assam required a rough and ready system of judicial administration, particularly in the hill areas. The new conquerors tried to utilise the existing judicial institutions like the panchayats retaining the final appelate jurisdiction for their officers. Gradually a system of code was prepared for the new province. Experiments and developments continued for the preparation of a uniform system together with other provinces of India. In 1861 Indian Civil Code and Indian Penal Code was introduced in the Assam Valley districts.

When the Chief Commissionership was created in 1874 no fundamental change was effected in the judicial administration in Assam. Practically judicial administration which had already been devised continued in the province. Thus the executive of officers of the Assam Valley continued to try civil and criminal cases, the jurisdiction of High Court of Calcutta was also retained over the judiciary of Assam. In the Surma Valley separate judicial staff was retained as they were during Bengal administration. Only in the Hill districts the Chief Commissioner was the highest court of appeal in criminal cases where the High Court did not have jurisdiction except over the Europeans.

Laws in Assam were the same as they were in other province of India. But for the Hill districts all the laws were not operative. There the Chief Commissioner with the approval of the government of India introduced some or parts of some laws while excluded others. Usually the village chiefs dispensed justice applying customery laws.

Judicial officers under the High Court dispensed justice. The help of assessors was taken by them in the Assam Valley districts but in the Surma Valley the jury system prevailed. Legal counsels could be had by both the contestants in disputes from professional legal practitioners.

The Administration of Police in Assam during the period had evolved out of the exigencies of the situation. When the first Police Stations were established they were modelled on the Bengal Administration. Over a large area one Station was set-up under an officer with few assistants. But gradually when troops were withdrawn from different parts of the country more stations had to be set-up, in many pläces outposts had to be opened.

In Assam proper, however, crime was rare and professional crime was almost negligible. But in the Hill districts and Frontier Tracts tribal disputes sometimes took violent shape. In such areas armed police had to be quartered. Thus besides Civil Police some quasi-military forces were also created for police purposes in the province. The Police Act of 1861 introduced in Assam laid the basis of police administration of the province.

After Assam became a Chief Commissionership, the province needed more security for development purpose, particularly, from the predatory hordes from hill tracts. Therefore, Frontier Police had to be geared up for protecting the border. Sometimes it became necessary to send punitive expeditions into the hills. Therefore Frontier Police Force was reorganised in 1882 to constitute Military Police. Subsequently the terms of service of the Military Police were assimilated with the Indian Army and in 1920 it was renamed Assam Rifles.

When Sylhet was added to Assam, the Police Force of the province faced another difficulty. Large waterlogged fields known as haors and beels were used by people as highway of commerce and transport. Robbers and smugglers in these areas could not be properly tackled by the Civil Police of the province. Moreover the long waterways of Brahmaputra required guards and the Steamer stations of ferry service necessitated a different police set-up. A new River Police force had to be created for this purpose.

In Assam proper, that is, in the Brahmaputra Valley districts and hills no village or Rural Police was provided. Policing in these areas was a local responsibility. The village chiefs recognised by the Government served to function in police purpose as well. But in permanently settled areas of Sylhet and Goalpara a system of Rural Police was provided by the enactment of Chowkidari acts. Some municipalities provided Chowkidars for police purposes.

Though usually for quite a long time police officers for Assam were taken on loan from Bengal and reverted to their home province after they became experienced, police force of the province had rendered on the whole good services to the country. Besides preventing and detecting crimes, they also helped in the management of roads, market places of public meeting, fairs, and protecting even the crops of the people by managing the cattle pounds. As the Police Commission recorded on the whole police administration of the province was efficient.

Thus we find that by 1920 the province of Assam took a definite shape along with other provinces of the British India, evolving from a crude beginning. The function of the Chief Commissioner's Government was to lay down broad and general principle for the guidance of its officers with due regard to the traditions of the province, but the functions of the Chief Commissioners, officers in Assam after 1912 had become formal and definite as in any province of British India. Though the administration lacked unity and symmetry althrough the province, yet it had assumed its final shape. The heterogenous character of both the people and administration of the province provided a unique example as to how diverse conditions could be brought under a single Government giving scope for mutual understanding and co-operation among the people, for the common good.

APPENDIX-A

LIST OF CHIEF COMMISSIONERS AND OTHER HEAD OF PROVINCE

Chief Commissioners of Assam

Colonel R.H. Keatinge, V.C., C.S.I.	:	1874 to 1878
Sir S.C. Bayley, K.C.S.I.	:	1878 to 1881
Sir C.A. Elliott, K.C.S.I.	:	1881 to 1885
Sir W.E. Ward, K.C.S I.*	:	1885 to 1887
Sir D. Fitzpatrick, K.C.S.I.	:	1887 to 1889
Mr. J.W. Quinton, C.S.I.	:	1889 to 1891
Sir W.F. Ward, K.C.S.I.	:	1891 to 1896
Sir H.J.S. Cotton, K.C.S.I.	:	1896 to 1902
Mr. J.B. Fuller, C.S.I., C.I.E.	:	1902 to 1905

Lieutenant-Governors of Eastern Bengal and Assam

Sir Bampfylde Fuller, K.C.S.I., K.C.I.E	:	1905 to 1906
Sir Lancelot Hare, K.C.S.I., K.C.I.E.	:	1906 to 1911
Sir Charles Bayley, K.C.S.I.	:	1911 to 1912

Chief Commissioners of Assam

Sir Archdale Earle, K.C.S.I., K.C.I.E.	:	1912 to 1918
Sir Nicholas Beatson Bell, K.C.S.I., K.C.I.E.	:	1918 to 1920

In addition to the above, there were several short officiating appointments, namely., Sir William Ward in 1883, Brigadier-General Collett, C.B. in 1891, Sir Charles Lyall, K.C.S.I. C.I.E., in 1894, Mr. Fuller in 1900, Mr. C.W. Bolton, C.S.I., in 1903, Col. P.R.T. Gordon, C.S.I., in 1914.

Officiating.

BIBLIOGRAPHY

Primary sources

Proceedings of the Government of Assam : General Department 1874-1922, Judicial Department 1874-1922, Revenue Department 1874-1922.

Proceedings of the Government of India : Home Public Department 1864-1922, Home Political Department 1864-1922, Home Police Department 1864-1922, Home Revenue Department 1864-1922, Home Judicial Department 1864-1922, Foreign Political Department 1864-1922, Home Establishment Department 1864-1922.

Report on the Administration of the Province of Assam : 1874-1905, 1912-1922.

Report on the Administration of Revenue in Assam : 1874-1905, 1912-1922.

Report on the Administration of Police in Assam : 1874-1905, 1912-1922.

Report on the Administration of Justice in Assam : 1874-1905, 1912-1922.

Resolution on the Administration of Revenue in Assam : 1880-1905, 1912-1922.

Resolution on the Administration of Police in Assam : 1880-1905, 1912-1922.

Resolution on the Administration of Justice in Assam : 1880-1905, 1912-1922

Administration Report of the Province of Eastern Bengal and Assam : 1905-1912.

Report on the Administration of Revenue, Eastern Bengal and Assam : 1905-1912.

Report on the Administration of Police, Eastern Bengal and Assam : 1905-1912.

Report on the Administration of Justice, Eastern Bengal and Assam : 1905-1912.

Assam Census Reports: 1881-1931.
Assam Valley Reassessment Report: 1892-93.
Assam Gazatteer : 1874-1920.
Report on the Indian Constitutional Reforms : 1919.
First Despatch on Indian Constitutional Reforms, 1919.
Report of the Indian Statutory Commission, Vol. I & II.
Assam Police Manual (Shillong, 1931), Reprinted in 1968.
Assam Land Revenue Manual (Calcutta, 1896), Reprinted in Shillong, 1965.
Assam Settlement Manual, Shillong, 1905.
Civil Justice Committee Report, 1925.
Indian Constitutional Statutes.
Report of the Royal Commision on Decentralization in India.
An account of the province of Assam and its administration, Shillong, 1903.
Assam Secretariat Manual, Shillong, 1903.
Manual of Executive Rules and Orders in Force in Assam, Shilong, 1903.
Manual of Secretariat Rules, Eastern Bengal and Assam, Shilllong, 1905.

Secondary sources

Allen, B.C. : Assam District Gazatteers, Shillong, 1906.
Aitchinson, C.U.: *Treaties, Engagements and Sanads*, Vol. II, Calcutta, 1909.
Buckland, C.E.: *Bengal under the Lieutenant-Governors*, 2 Vols., Calcutta, 1901.
Butler, T.: *A Sketch of Assam with some Account of the Hill Tribes by an Officer*, London, 1874.
Bailey, F.M.: *China-Tibet-Assam*, London, 1945.
Baden-Powell, B.H.: *Land System of British India*, Vol. III, Oxford, 1892.
Banerjee, A.C.: *The North East Frontier of India*, Calcutta, 1946.
Barpuzari, H.K.: *Assam in the Days of Company*, Gauhati, 1964.
Bhuyan, S.K.: *Anglo-Assamese Relations 1771-1826*, Gauhati, Assam, 1949
Bishop, S.O.: *Sketches in Assam*, Calcutta, 1885.
Chakraborty, B.C.: *British Relations with Hill Tribes*, Calcutta, 1964.

Curzon, Lord.: *British Government in India*, 2 Vols., London, 1925.

Dutt, K.N.: *A Handbook to the Old Records of Assam Secretariat*, Shillong, 1959.

Dutt, K.N.: *Land Marks of the Freedom Movement in Assam*, Gauhati, 1958.

Gait, E.: *A History of Assam* (Calcutta, 1905), 3rd edited reprint, Gauhati, 1967.

Holdich, T.H.: *The Indian Borderland*, London, 1901.

Hamilton Francis: *An Account of Assam*, Gauhati, 1940.

Hunter, W.W.: *The Imperial Gazeetteer of India*, Vol. IV & VI. *A Statistical Account of Assam*, Calcutta, 1879.

Ilbert, Courtney: *The Government of India*, London, 1915.

Johnstone, Sir J.: *Captain Welsh's Expedition to Assam 1992-94*, London, 1912.

Kaye, W.J.: *The Administration of the East India Company* (London, 1853) edited print, Allahabad, 1966

Keith, A.B.: *A Constitutional History of India*, London, 1936.

Lahiri, R.M.: *Annexamina of Assam*, Calcutta, 1954.

Misra, B.B.: *The Central Administration of the East India Campany*, Bombay, 1959.

Mill, J.A.M.: *Report on the Province of Assam*, Calcutta, 1854.

Mukherjee, P.: *Indian Constitutional Documents*, 2nd Calcutta, 1918.

Mackenzie, A.: *History of the Relations of Government with the Hill Tribes of the North East Frontier of Bengal*, Calcutta, 1884.

Memorandum on the North East Frontier of Bengal, Calcutta, 1869.

Prasad, B.: *The Origin of Provincial Autonomy*, Allahabad, 1941.

Pemberton, R.B.: *Report on the Eastern Frontier of British India*, Calcutta, 1835.

Palande, M.R.: *Indian Administration*, London, 1947.

Reid, A.S.: *Chin-Lushai Land*, Calcutta, 1893.

Reid, R.: *History of the Frontier Areas Bordering on Assam from 1883-1941*, Shillong, 1942.

Rao, V. Venkata: *Hundred Years of Local Self-government* (Gauhati, 1963), 2nd edition, 1965.

Rustomiji, N.K.: *Tribal Administration in the North East Frontier Agency*, Delhi, 1955.

Shakespeare, L.W.: *History of the Assam Rifles*, London, 1929.

Shakespeare, L.W.: *History of Upper Assam, Upper Burma, North Eastern Frontier*, London, 1914.

Saikia, K.N.: *Assam Land Revenue Regulation*, 1886, Gauhati, 1965.

Ward, G.L.S.: *Assam Adventure*, London, 1942.

Waddel, L.A.: *The Tribes of the Brahmaputra Valley*, Calcutta, 1901.

Wade, T.P.: *Geographical Sketch of Assam*, 1880, Asiatic Annual Register, London 1805.

Wilcox, R.: Memoir of a Survey of Assam and the neighbouring Countries, *Asiatic Research*, Calcutta, Vol. XVII.

Verrier Elwin: *India's North East Frontier*, London, 1959.

Woodthrope, R.G.: *The Lushai Expedition 1871-72*, London, 1873, Assam Surveys 1877-78, Simla, 1878, *The Naga Hills Expedition*, London, 1877.

Young, E.C.: A Journey from Yunan to Assam, *Geographical Journal*, London, Vol. XXX, 1907.

INDEX